PRAISE FOR *DANCE IT OUT GIRL*

"This book is packed to the brim  women all need to hear at one ti. lifetime. I know you will enjoy this comfort and wisdom in knowing th ᴜwɪɪ battles, but we are not without the ᵖ... ᵖ.ᴄ or the tools to see us through. The phrase "it takes a village" is ever so true in my life."

Brittney Crawford

Homemaker and a mom of four

"Shannon currently lives in the trenches of motherhood. As a mother, wife, daughter, sister, friend, therapist, and author, she is authentically living out the reality of what real motherhood looks like. Join her in the midst of her beautiful mess and rest easy, dear mommies, you are not alone! Join her for a journey leading into authentic living and intentional self-kindness. You will not be disappointed!"

Christina Kavenagh

Licensed mental health counselor at Five Stones
Counseling Services, LLC and a mom of two

"Once you start reading any of Shannon's books, you won't want to put them down. Shannon is super transparent, relatable, and oh, so very helpful."

Laura Rhines

Licensed marriage and family therapist at Coffee and
Change Counseling, LLC and a mom of two

"Shannon has the ability to relate to moms from a variety of backgrounds. It's not just being able to relate but the gift of making every parent that she comes in contact with feel like they are valued, that they are important to their family and have self-worth. Shannon has inspired me personally to live every day not as a perfect parent but as a loving, nurturing, and perfectly imperfect mom."

Shawn Middleton
Homemaker and a mom of twins

"Shannon is transparent in her approach to writing, so much so that you will feel like you are personally hearing her speak the words on the page to you. Shannon is an incredible writer, an incredible counselor, and most importantly to me, an incredible friend and mentor. You will not be disappointed you made the choice to hear her words."

Robert J. Hovel, Jr.
AP Psychology instructor at Lyman High School

"The internal struggles and frequent chaos that Shannon faces daily can range from comical situations to dark self-doubt and struggles. She knows life as a working mother is very real, and she strives to have the good times outweigh the challenging times. I have watched her utilize her skills to not only mold her own children but to help grieving young children and troubled teens as well. Shannon swims through the muck of life and continues to shine as an accomplished and amazing human being."

Joan Spears
Instructional reading coach at the Seminole County
School District and a mom of two

"Shannon is not only a remarkable mother, wife, and licensed mental health counselor but now an amazing author! Sharing her incredible journey will help other young mothers. I am so proud to know her."

Gail Benson
Owner of the Look Salon and BlowDry Bar

"*Dance It Out Girl* is a delightful read. Shannon offers a refreshingly honest, humorous, and "no holds barred" description of her experiences and insights about what it is really like to be a mom. Her words will cause a sigh of relief to moms everywhere who are struggling to live up to the perfect motherhood myth!"

Sherrie Sitarik
Former CEO of Orlando Health and a mom of two

"Sometimes all you have to do is give yourself permission. So do it! Allow yourself permission to take a break, sit back, put your feet up, relax, and read a book that will speak to your soul. You aren't alone, and you aren't the only one struggling with day-to-day life. Being a parent is rewarding, but it's also exhausting. This book helps you to recognize that we all deal with similar issues, and as soon as we realize that, we will feel empowered and become our best self."

Emily Mohabir
Registered nurse at Parrish Medical Center and a mom of four

"After reading *Dance It Out, Girl!*, it feels like your bestie is talking you through the challenges of life. It doesn't matter what stage you are going through in this beautiful yet messy life. This book can and will relate to you. If you are a mom, a stepmother, or a woman just trying to find yourself, this book will help not just you but everyone around you. Just give it a shot. I'm glad I did."

Laura Johnson
Homemaker and a mom of two

"*Dance It Out, Girl!* is a refreshing portrayal of the ups and downs of motherhood. As a mother of four and a licensed mental health counselor, Shannon Rowell combines her professional training and personal experiences as a mother to write a fantastic book about the psychological, emotional, and physical joys and struggles that we, as mothers, constantly juggle."

Emily Martucci
Homemaker and a mom of three

"*Dance It Out, Girl!* is a compilation of the great advice you need from a counselor, the good vibes and support you want from a fellow mama, and the honesty you get from your best friend. Shannon beautifully guides us through the emotions that can creep up as you journey through motherhood. This book would have been such a blessing in the early stages of raising my children as a mama of three. Now, I utilize these techniques as I navigate the teenage years, while also running a successful apparel brand. I have learned to embrace today; to walk in my purpose, on purpose; to accept that I am perfectly imperfect, and I wish the same for you."

April Mae Guenther
Owner of SandiLake Clothing and a mom of three

"Becoming a mom changes your world in thousands of ways. Growing a cape of magical superpowers is not one of them, and Shannon will be the first to let you know. As a skilled mom of four, Shannon knows the exhausting challenges that encompass being a mom and has a way of putting you at ease. She's a wonderful therapist and it reflects in her craft."

Ashley McDaniel
Coordinator of Risk Prevention at the University
of Central Florida and a mom of two

I have had the honor and joy of delivering all four of Shannon's beautiful babies. The experiences she shares in this book are reflective of what I hear from so many mothers, yet her perspective is unique and insightful. Anyone who is a mother will find the humor and commonality shared in *Dance It Out, Girl!*

Sanjay Tandon, MD

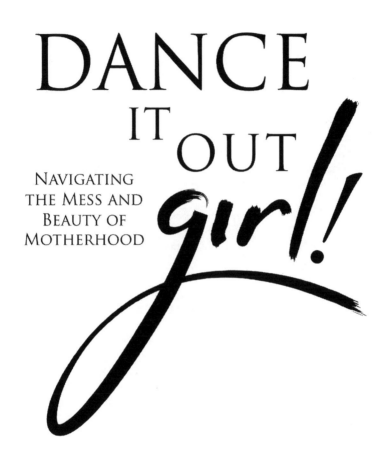

DANCE
IT OUT
girl!

NAVIGATING
THE MESS AND
BEAUTY OF
MOTHERHOOD

SHANNON LEIGH ROWELL

Dance It Out Girl: Navigating the Mess and Beauty of Motherhood
By Shannon Leigh Rowell

Published by HigherLife Developmental Services, Inc.
PO Box 623307
Oviedo, Fl 32765
407.463.4806
www.ahigherlife.com

Disclaimer: All accounts shared in this book have been done so with individual consent. Some names and identifying details have been changed to protect the privacy of these individuals.

Unless otherwise noted, Scripture quotations are from *The Holy Bible: NEW INTERNATIONAL VERSION®*. Copyright ©1973, 1978, 1984 by Biblica, Inc. All rights reserved worldwide. Used by permission.

Paperback ISBN: 978-1-7332289-0-9
eBook ISBN: 978-1-7332289-1-6

Editor: Kimberly See, Editing with Love
Cover Design: Fiona Jayde, Fiona Jayde Media
Interior Design: Tamara Cribley, The Deliberate Page

First Edition

Printed in the United States of America

As much as I would love to dedicate this book to so many people, there is one little one who inspired me the most to write this book. I dedicate this book to my daughter, Arleigh Lynn.

From the moment I found out I was pregnant I knew there was something different about you. From the start, you were a little fighter, and even with so many complications, you fought your way into this world. You have taught me to fight and reach for my dreams despite the obstacles I might come across. I am so thankful for your courageous little spirit. I know God has big plans for your life. All the love, my sweet Arleigh.

I would also like to recognize my husband, Steve, and my other three amazing children. The amount of love and support you have given me has made me a better person. I love doing life together and wouldn't have wanted to reach this goal without you. Thank you, my loves.

TABLE OF CONTENTS

INTRODUCTION

This wasn't my first rodeo. I had successfully pushed three babies out of me before, so I knew I was capable of delivering our fourth and final baby girl. What I wasn't prepared for was the intensity of the emotions and triggers this birth experience would bring, because of some of my past traumas.

I began to cry uncontrollably as, what felt like, twenty-some people entered the delivery room after I heard the words, "C-section, STAT." I clung to my husband's hand as we were being ripped apart by a team of people pulling my bed into the hallway. I heard the anesthesiologist tell my doctor that she didn't have the time to get the numbing medicine inside my body and that she would do the injection in the surgical room. I was terrified as they strapped me down to a table and pumped medicine through my veins. I was freezing and so scared my baby girl wasn't going to make it. A couple seconds later, I heard a faint cry, and then I threw up everywhere. What an awesome way to bring a life into this world.

In the months to follow, I fell into a dark place. I was depressed. I was having flashbacks of past abuse. From my C-section scar that just never seemed to stop hurting, I was reminded daily of past instances of self-harm. It was during this time that I realized I needed to get some help. Of course, being a counselor myself and having thoughts of needing to find my own counselor was frightening. I didn't know if I would be looked at as being weak, unable to help myself out of this dark space. Counseling, after all, was my career and I should know how to help myself. I did eventually find a counselor, but I gave her my maiden name just in case she ever decided to google me. It took me a while before I eventually told her who I was. It was relieving to be validated, to be told that everyone needs a little help sometimes.

In addition to seeking help from a counselor, I found another amazing way to cope when I was feeling down: dancing in my living room. I would turn the music up and just start moving. Soon this became a regular part of our family's way of shaking off the blues. We call it "dancing it out."

After my birth experience, I realized that I am not alone. There are people out there who are afraid to seek help and guidance in a time of need. There are people out there who are not able to afford to see a counselor regularly. Through these next several pages, it is my goal and desire to help you so that you, too, can gain better skills and some encouragement to help you where you are in your life. I want to encourage you to let others into your life who will help lift you up and support you.

The last book I wrote, Chains Be Broken: Finding Freedom from Cutting, Anxiety, Depression, Anorexia and Suicide, was definitely a little more intense than I intend this book to be. This book outlines my story as a teenager where I speak about the struggles that I have experienced and how I overcame them, mostly. Since my teenage years, I have learned so many life lessons that have helped me become the person I am today. I would like the words on these pages to be of inspiration and motivation.

I wrote this book to be geared toward young mothers because, well, I would like to think I am a young mother too. I have gone through some rough patches but have somehow navigated them okay, so far. I hope this book will help lift and encourage you as you navigate through life's messy but beautiful experiences that shape you into the person you were meant to become.

Commit to the Lord whatever you do
and your plans will succeed.[1]

Proverbs 16:3

CHAPTER ONE

Perfectly Imperfect

I'm dressed to the nines with my skinny jeans and long black boots. My black lace shirt is layered over a cute tank top. My hair is blonde and flowing freely through the wind. My wrist is adorned with my beautiful Alex and Ani bracelets that display each of my kids' birthstones. My heels are five inches tall and I walk flawlessly in them. I'm perfectly put together with not a hair out of place.... Who am I kidding? In reality, I am curled up on the couch, wearing my comfy black floral yoga pants and a tank top. I am also wearing a cover-up because, well, let's face it, I'm not wearing a bra. I hate them and would rather not feel restricted, at least when I am home.

I used to think I had to be perfect—okay, at least almost perfect. It all started at a young age, when I felt the need to have to please anyone and everyone. I strived to get good grades at all times. I tried to never let anyone down. I realized much later in my life—and when I say later, I mean as an adult—that by trying to be "perfect" or by trying to fit into the mold of what others wanted me to be, I was only making other people happy and not necessarily myself. I don't see the point in that now.

I would think, maybe if I were thin enough, people would listen to and respect me. Maybe if I conformed to professional standards, people would believe I knew what I was talking about as a mental health counselor. I also used to think I was too young to counsel others older than me, and I would feel insecure about it. You know what, though, I'm pretty confident in my abilities. Not just my abilities as a professional but my abilities as a mother, wife, daughter, and friend. I enjoy helping other people. I also enjoy being myself and not having to compromise myself.

For instance, I love not having to dress up when I go into the office. There were so many times growing up when I would be seen by a professional, and they would be wearing "work clothes." This only made me feel like I had nothing in common with them or that they wouldn't be able to help me because they would never be able to understand or relate to me. Granted, I primarily work with teenagers and young adults now, so dressing down has only been an advantage in being able to relate to my clients. I'm also mostly around my kids, so having pink in my hair, even if it is just extensions, gives me even more clout. My clients and children see me and love me for who I am, not who others expect me to be.

I am made to be perfectly imperfect and so are you.

The first time I felt comfortable around an adult, I was in counseling with a male counselor for an eating disorder that I started to develop. The counselor walked in, plopped himself into a chair, and threw off his shoes while also taking off his tie. At first, I was taken back and didn't know what the heck was going on. He just started talking to me like a friend, not as an adult but someone who seemed to understand me a little. This little gesture meant a lot to me. I try to use the same informal persona now in my practice.

When I was younger, my mother would come home from work, and she would be dressed to the nines. My family life felt so formal and it was hard for me to be myself. Finally, my mom started to change out of her work clothes when she came home from working all day, and that little change made things at home more informal and more comfortable for me.

I am made to be perfectly imperfect and so are you. This world would be so boring if we were all the same or like-minded. Being different is what allows us to be the best versions of ourselves. We continue to be shaped by our experiences, whether they are positive or negative. It is how we cope and make the most out of our experiences that continue to shape us into the people we are meant to become.

As a counselor, I have encountered many individuals who were suffering from dissociative identity disorder. They had suffered from multiple traumas, and as a result of not being able to cope, they would split their person- alities. After my first experience with treating dissociative iden- tity disorder, I made sure I was the one sitting closest to the *I am not perfect, and my life does not have to look perfect to be a "perfect" life for me and my family.* exit door. With split personalities, you never know which one you're speaking to and what they will do.

It might seem like it would be a welcome break, to be able to split up your personality. In doing so, you wouldn't have to deal with all of life's stressors at the same time. It would be another break if you could separate the parts of you that experiences grief, trauma, pain, work, and friends and family life. To some people, it might seem that, in being able to do these splits, life would seem more manageable. It can seem easier, but the truth is, we experience these things as a whole because they make us who we are as individuals. A lot of times, we can't deal with life or it becomes so overwhelming because we weren't given the proper tools to help us cope. It's never too late to start learning or to ask for help.

While I was pregnant, I developed such severe anxiety that I wasn't able to leave my house. Every time I left, I felt like something bad would happen, like getting bad news about my baby girl not growing properly or some bad news about my health. I started to become irrational in my thinking. I thought that if I only got bad news when I left my house, then maybe I could prevent the bad from happening by staying alone and in my comfort zone, my home. Of course, this didn't work because eventually, my baby had to come out. I sure wasn't going to try to be a hero and give birth at home. After my little princess was born, it felt like more and more bad things continued to happen. I started to realize I couldn't do it all on my own. After the birth of my previous baby, I developed postpartum depression and post-traumatic stress disorder. The delivery of my baby girl was a trigger to some of my past traumas.

Let me preface this by saying that I have never liked relying on other people. I'm not sure who really does. The week following my little girl's birth, I was pretty much in the neonatal intensive care unit (NICU) with her every day, and I had to rely on others to help me with everything else in my life. I felt like I was falling apart. I felt like I was also opening myself up to judgment from others. In my mind, that's what having to rely on others meant. We all know people can have some strong opinions, and some of them are not always nice. I'm not entirely sure what I felt I would be judged on, however, I just didn't need the extra pressure at the time. The feeling of judgment can be challenging to add to our everyday lives. We should all work together to ensure we are not adding this stress to others.

I know I don't sit around judging others so I'm not sure why I would I think someone is doing this to me. My husband and I often like to saddle up our bikes and head out with the kids on a long bike ride. It's quite a sight to be seen: my husband with our baby on his bike, me with our toddler on my bike, and the two older kids riding their own bikes. During one of our bike rides through our neighborhood, we spotted a young girl, one of the kids' friends. She was helping her brother take care of a family dog while the dog's family was out of town. She was running on the sidewalk, and as she saw us, she commented loudly, "I'm still in my pajamas. Don't judge me."

I thought to myself, Don't judge me? Are you kidding me? This was an eight-year-old girl on winter break. She was just a kid! I hate that she even thought we would think badly or any differently of her because she was comfortable in her pajamas. I have to be honest, half the time I live in my yoga clothes. They're great because they could be considered either pajamas or daywear.

Have you ever seen the movie Daddy's Home 2? The main character is recently divorced and has remarried. The new wife, who looks like a model, is constantly jotting things down in a tiny notebook everywhere she goes. In one of the scenes, the ex-wife is in the kitchen, yelling at one of her kids. She looks over and sees her ex-husband's new wife looking at her and writing in her notebook. Of course, the ex-wife automatically assumes she is writing something judgmental about her parenting skills. The ex-wife snaps a quick, sarcastic response at her. Toward the end of the movie, though, they both share a sweet moment when the new wife hands over the notebook for the ex-wife to read. The ex-wife is surprised in seeing that every word about her is something positive she has done in motherhood or in her daily life. Imagine the amazing feeling she felt after reading positive traits that someone else saw in her.

Judgment is defined as the way in which people develop their opinions of others through the use of comparison. Nowhere in this statement does it suggest that judgment is meant to be negative. I'm not sure why we tend to assume we are being judged negatively. Granted, most of the time, when I think of judgment, I think of the negative too, but it doesn't have to be that way. How cool would it be if we lifted each other up for the wonderful things we are doing, without pulling each other down?

This reminds me of when I moved out of my parents' house. I found myself starting to do little things that my parents would do, like vacuum a lot. I was constantly cleaning and tidying up. While I lived with my parents, they usually kept the house pretty clean and clutter-free. After I started having kids, especially after my fourth child, these tasks became a lot more difficult. Anytime my parents would visit my house or see the inside of my car, I would cringe. In fact, I tried to clean and declutter before I would see them, but it didn't always work out that way. Now, I have just come to accept that I live in a house with six people, four of whom are young kids. The second I pick up the house, it's not long before it's cluttered again. When people come over now, I try to embrace the mess if I don't get to clean up before they arrive. And this is OKAY! I am not perfect, and my life does not have to look perfect to be a "perfect" life for me and my family.

We all have different styles and sets of skills that make us unique. I love that I have a friend who can work part-time from home and homeschool all four of her children at the same time. Bless this mama because she almost never gets a break. I love another mama who chooses to put her children in private school and spends her time volunteering and shuttling kids to and from baseball practice almost every single day.

I'm not a perfect parent by any means. Once, when my two-year-old daughter was at my parents' house, she dropped her baby doll on the ground. The next word that came out of her sweet, little mouth was, well, a not so nice four letter word I'm sure she has heard me say too. In fact, I'm pretty sure that's where she got the expression from. I didn't know if I should have been mortified that my daughter had just cursed in front of my parents (who don't ever curse) or to laugh a little because, well, at least she used it in the correct context. So I laughed and shrugged it off because I'm not perfect, she's not perfect, and life happens. I wasn't even concerned with feeling judged at that moment. I chose to embrace the chaos instead and shrugged it off.

I ask you to please not strive to be perfect in everything you do; of course you should give it your all, but if you strive to be perfect, you will inevitably fail. When you are too busy worrying about having a clean house, well put together children, a gourmet meal cooked every night of the week, and laundry always clean, folded and put away, then you are missing out. You are missing out on the most important moment, and that's the moment you are currently living in. It's not our faults either that we feel this immense pressure to have to be everything and do it all. We have been conditioned from a young age to listen to the negative statements we hear about ourselves. We listen to our negative cognitions and react accordingly to the negative thoughts that society's pressure has put on us. So, to all the moms out there, from the picture-perfect Pinterest mom to the one struggling just to get her kids out the door in the morning (that's me, by the way): You are amazing!! I praise you and want to tell you that you are doing exactly what you were designed to do for your children. You are a blessing to your children.

Our Beautiful Mess

Dear family and friends,
We may look like a mess
In the chaos that we live in,
Have stains on our clothes or
Hair in a frizz.

We may have toys from here to there,
Have a kitchen that needs care,
Or things needing tending too
Put on hold without a care.

Homework, baths, dinner, and bottles.
A room full of laundry
That we can get to tomorrow.

A life we live largely and thank God for each day,
A family blessed with six
That is loved and cared for in each and every way.

Love and laughter fill our hearts and home.
A grateful mess,
Because without it, our family would not feel whole.

So we embrace this time given to us.
We live and love endlessly
Because one day we will sit here, only
Just us two,
Wishing we could go back to the chaos we once knew.

CHAPTER TWO

I Just Can't, or Can I?

I looked myself up and down in the long mirror hanging in my room. I focused in on my eyes. I felt like the eyes that were looking back at me were that of another person. I felt extreme hatred. I saw a girl with small breasts, love handles, and a big bootie. I told myself I wasn't beautiful, that I was too fat to be loved by anyone, that I would never get married in this ugly skin. It was the beginning of my journey to anorexia.

Every experience we have in life will either tells us something positive or something negative about who we think we really are inside. Unfortunately, negative thoughts do tend to stay with us longer than any positive thoughts.

In my sessions, I love to do an activity where my clients write out their life timeline. I ask them to start with the earliest memory they can remember and work their way to their current age. Some memories will be good, some memories will be bad, and others may just be neutral.

With each negative memory, we also tend to tell ourselves something negative about ourselves. For instance, let's say your parents divorced when you were young. A negative thought you might have told yourself is, "It's all my fault." Now let's say, years down the road, your own long-term relationship ends and you have those same feelings come up again. "It's all my fault," you tell yourself. The more times you hear the same negative message, the more your brain believes it. It becomes instilled into who you believe you are as a person.

For every one negative message said to you, at least five positive messages are needed to counteract it. Most of the time, we are not even aware of all the negative messages we tell ourselves. I'm not good enough. I'm unworthy to be loved. I'm too young to be taken seriously. Through the use of self-awareness and a simple life timeline, you can make yourself more aware of the types of messages you tell yourself. You then have the ability to turn them around to be more positive messages in your life.

Think about it this way: You wouldn't want to be friends with someone who was constantly putting you down or telling you that you're not good enough. So we shouldn't allow ourselves to say those negative messages to ourselves either. If anything, we need to be the kindest version of ourselves to ourselves.

...we need to be the kindest version of ourselves to ourselves. We need to give ourselves grace.

We need to give ourselves grace. There is enough negativity in the world; let's not add to it by believing our own negative thoughts about ourselves.

When packing my kids lunches for school, I've tried to make it a point to write a little note in their lunchbox as an encouragement for them to speak their own positives into their lives. I want them to know how much they are loved and how they are worthy to be loved! I remind them that they are amazing. I remind them that they can make a positive difference in the lives of others. Just think, if we can change our child's day around with a simple note in their lunchbox, imagine what else we can do, what else they will be able to do.

This isn't to say that we are always going to be positive, but if we start with ourselves, eventually, we can pour positivity into others. I know some of you are thinking that with all the daily struggles we experience, it can be difficult to stay positive. While this is true, a skill called mindfulness can be implemented to help.

Practicing mindfulness is maintaining a non-judgmental state of mind and having a heightened awareness of our thoughts, emotions, and experiences. The definition is a little bit of a mouth full, so let's break it down. A lot of times, we are not aware of our surroundings because we are also not fully aware of the emotions our surroundings invite. For example, my kids—and husband, for that matter—can be very messy. When they are eating dinner or doing some other activity in the kitchen, I try to minimize the mess by cleaning up as I go. I know, for me, that the more mess and the more clutter around me, the more I will experience anxiety. When one of my kids accidentally drops their cup of milk or sprite all over the floor, I can choose to react in one of two ways. I can yell and get upset because there is yet another mess for me to clean, or I can calmly state that it's okay because it was just an accident and it's an easy cleanup.

It is important to remember that accidents will happen, and it's not the end of the world.

I would like to say I always choose the calmer method, but truthfully, we are all human. I can get frustrated just as easily as anyone else. It's not until I take a moment before I react to consider the emotion I am feeling. The emotions I choose, deciding whether to have a positive or negative reaction, will impact my kids' day more than mine. When I yell, I am displaying anger for my kids to mimic, and this teaches them an unhealthy way of coping.

When I am calm, I am practicing being mindful in the moment and teaching my kids a valuable lesson in controlling their emotions. It is important to remember that accidents will happen, and it's not the end of the world. This is not to say that I will always respond perfectly because we all know I won't, and neither will you. Even on the days when I don't respond well, it allows me the opportunity to apologize to my kids. This allows me to figure out what I was feeling in the moment, which then normalizes feeling big emotions. It is a win-win!

When I was dating my husband in college, I had absolutely no concept of mindfulness. I was riding in his truck, which he really loved, and I accidentally dropped my hot coffee all over his seat. I was so embarrassed. I tried to find a towel to clean it up, but I didn't know where to look. All I could do was apologize profusely. I thought for sure, as soon as I looked up at his face, that he would be livid with me. When I finally looked up, I was surprised to see that he was smiling at me. He told me it wasn't that big of a deal and could be easily cleaned up. I was floored! I mean, coffee is not an easy smell to get rid of.

The compassion and control of emotions he showed me that day revealed to me that I could probably do the same. I now strive to take a step back in stressful moments to first figure out how I am feeling, and then decide how I want to react. During those moments, I am not only being mindful, I am reminding myself to have grace.

One of the hardest parts of being mindful is intentionally trying to be fully present in the moment and paying attention to your surroundings. I love looking up to the sky and observing the clouds. I love trying to find images out of the clouds to see what I can make up in my mind. Doing this simple exercise allows me a break, to be present in nature—the nature God created for us to enjoy. Being intentionally present isn't always easy, but it does become easier once you have experienced someone else's undivided attention. It might mean putting down your electronics in the evening to enjoy some family time. It might mean playing a game with someone instead of watching a movie. When we are intentionally present while with others, we show them how much we value them. We show them they are worthy of our time and attention.

Techniques for being mindful: These are just a few ways you can become mindful of yourself and your surroundings. It is important that we take care of ourselves, if not daily then a little each week, so we can be fully present when caring for ourselves and our loved ones.

Breathe: I love the application on the Apple Watch that stops you in your tracks to remind you to breathe. Take a couple moments each day to stop and feel your breath move in and out of you, and allow yourself to relax with each exhale.

Live in the moment: Put all distractions away. Put away the computer and the phone. Turn off the television or hide the remote for a few hours. Forget the loads of laundry or piles of dirt on the floor. Instead, engage with whoever is around you and be fully present.

Meditation: Okay, I don't mean sitting with your legs crossed, hands palms up and chanting OHM. I simply want you to take a moment for yourself. Concentrate on any tightness or aches and pains you may feel throughout your body. Once you identify the tension, you can focus on releasing the unpleasant feeling and letting it fade away.

Go for a walk: There are so many great benefits to walking. Not only does it boost your serotonin (the good-feeling hormones) levels, but it also allows you to slow down and process information. As you walk, you tend to look around, and when your eyes move back and forth, it actually signals your brain to process information that was once stagnant. This is a great way to relieve stress as well as process some things and get some exercise.

CHAPTER THREE

You are Good Enough

There are plenty of times when I have felt like I wasn't good enough. I'm not a good enough mom, I'm not a good enough friend, I'm not a good enough parent. And the list can go on. We have all had these thoughts at some point in our lives, but the truth is, you are good enough. In Psalm 139:14, it says, "I praise you because you are fearfully and wonderfully made; your works are wonderful, I know that full well."[1] That means you were made in God's image. God is perfect, and He made you to be good enough from the start.

In my early twenties, I was working full time at an entry-level job. During this time, I was also working part-time as an intern in the counseling field, going to graduate school to finish my degree in mental health counseling, writing my first book, and was pregnant with my first baby. Even with all of these wonderful things going on in my life, I was sad. I often felt like I wasn't good enough to be any of those things: a student, an intern, an author, or a new mother.

I learned so much during my time at my internship and felt very confident in my abilities. However, at my full-time job, which was not in the counseling field, I often felt insecure. I realized I only felt insecure around the people who were above me and had higher credentials than I did. I thought at the time that I wasn't as good as they were. I didn't have any credentials in their line of work (fundraising) and certainly none behind my name yet within the mental health counseling field I was studying.

Nothing could have been further from the truth. I just didn't realize, as my young naïve self wouldn't have at the time, that it is not about credentials but about the knowledge and experience you gain along the way. During this time, I also realized that everyone has insecurities. I have insecurities. You have insecurities. The doctor you go to for help when you are sick has insecurities. The put together mother down the road has insecurities. The difference in knowing who is struggling and who is confident in their insecurities comes from finding out who can hide their insecurities better. It is okay to be vulnerable and share your insecurities. You never know who you can help by sharing what is going on in your life. How you use your skills and experiences to help others is what really matters, so be confident in what you are doing.

It's okay to stay on your path. Know what is important and keep going.

I could have gone straight to doctoral school after I graduated from my Master's program. I would have been Dr. Shannon Leigh Rowell. Oooh, I love the sound of that! However, it wouldn't have helped me benefit others any more than my current credentials as a licensed mental health counselor. I would have ended up spending more money to be a "doctor" without a guarantee of making more money or helping others in a bigger way than I do now. It's okay to stay on your path. Know what is important and keep going.

Whether you are a high school graduate, an entrepreneur, someone with a title such as a lawyer or a doctor, or even a full-time stay-at-home parent, know that you are good enough. You are exactly where you need to be. You are helping others in the capacity you were created for during the season you are in.

As a young girl, I used to think my parents were invincible and couldn't do anything wrong. I mean, I knew that they had to make some mistakes, but I never saw them do anything blatantly wrong. It wasn't until I was much older that I finally realized my parents' way of doing things wasn't always what I believed was the right way. I started to develop my own opinions. This helped me gain more confidence to become my own person. Of course, I have kept a lot of the fundamentals they taught me, but I am making my own fundamentals now as a mother, wife, friend, etc.

After realizing that the most influential adults in your life also make mistakes, you start to also realize that we aren't all that different after all. That makes you and everyone else equal. We are essentially the same, no different fundamentally. What's that saying? We all put our pants on one leg at a time. The next time you find yourself questioning your abilities or feeling inadequate next to someone else, just remember that they, too, have insecurities. They are trying to get through life just as you are.

A friend once told me, quoting Dr. Bernard Baruch, "Be who you are and say what you feel because those who mind don't matter and those who matter don't mind."[2] Wow, I don't know about you, but those words ring true for me. So often we try to please other people. We try to "fit in" with the crowd, but we are only doing a disservice to ourselves and others around us by trying to fit in. Think about how much each of us has to offer to those around us, yet half the time, we hold back and choose to conform instead. I love asking people how they are feeling. It's a question that often catches them off guard. Instead of focusing on how they feel, they are forced to shift that into the question of how they are doing. Most of the time, I get a one-word answer: Fine. That word is a red flag for me! When someone tells me that they are doing fine, I usually tell them the acronym for what I believe the word "fine" means. F for an unfortunately bad four lettered word, I for insane, N for nevertheless, and E for emotional. Usually, after I explain how I think they are feeling based on their response, they will nod in agreement. It so hard for a lot of us to be truthful with others about how we are feeling. It can make people feel like they look weak and more open to their vulnerabilities.

It works the other way around as well. It is funny how fast you can make someone feel uncomfortable when you really respond with how you are feeling. Most of the time, people are perplexed when others respond with their true feelings, especially when these feelings are negative. In reality, feelings are all apart of our basic makeup. We weren't created to be robots. We don't have to put on a stone-cold face because we are afraid to express ourselves for fear of what others might think. There is no need to feel guilty for feeling certain emotions.

I know it's not always easy for us to accept ourselves. I, for one, am guilty of this. We have to decide that we should never have to hide who we are out of fear or guilt or shame from others. I can't tell you how many times I see moms guilted into thinking they are horrible mothers because they choose to parent differently than their peers. I see clichés in which friends refuse to let outsiders in because they might not fit into their "style." I believe that no one should ever make you feel guilty for being you. You do not have to change who you are or do something you do not want to do because someone has made you feel guilty.

> *If you haven't done so already, take the time to talk to a friend who you can lean on when times get hard.*

I used to feel guilty if I wasn't constantly helping other people. I became the "go-to person" for a lot of people because I would always say yes. I would say yes to just about anything. I committed to attending events hours away from home, watching extra kids, and going to dinner with girlfriends when I would have rathered stay home. I got so tired and burnt out from overcommitting myself all of the time.

A friend of mine once told me how guilty she felt when she didn't come through for her friends. She also came to the same realization that she just couldn't always overcommit herself. Having said this, she also reminded me of a time when she and I were both depressed. Instead of saying no to others and setting healthy boundaries, we ended up saying no to isolate ourselves. It can be so easy to do this to yourself when you're feeling sad, even if it is not always the best decision.

Luckily, she and I had each other. We could always sense when the other was sad and just wanted to be alone. When this happened, we didn't let each other sit and wallow. If you haven't done so already, take the time to talk to a friend who you can lean on when times get hard. Let them know when you are really struggling. I encourage you—if you are struggling with depression, anxiety, or any other mental illness—to reach out to someone. Reach out to a friend, a caregiver, a co-worker, or, most importantly, a counselor. I promise you won't regret reaching out to someone when you need it most.

One year, I decided my new word would be No. I wouldn't say no every time, but I would instead choose to say no to the things I really didn't want to do. I wouldn't allow myself to feel guilty anymore over not saying yes and helping everyone with everything. I have to say that saying no feels better than I ever would have expected.

For years I have taught my clients how to set healthy boundaries, although I had not been setting any myself. When you set healthy boundaries with others, you are clarifying your expectations and being consistent about enforcing your expectations. A couple of things that I have personally had to set boundaries around are birthday parties, family time, and self-care. It may sound a little silly to some people, so let me explain.

I absolutely hate kids birthday parties. I don't know what it is about going to them, I just can't stand them. I have always done a birthday party for my kids' first birthdays and have gone all-out. Beyond that, we only celebrate with family celebrations each subsequent birthday. If my kids want to attend a birthday party, I try to wait until they are old enough to be dropped off and picked up. My friends are finally starting to understand that if they invite my kids to their kids' birthday parties, they probably won't be going. It doesn't mean we will stiff them on their gift, though.

I also love my family time. I prefer to have uninterrupted family moments, from the time my husband walks in the door until my kids go to bed. My husband and I really have to work on being intentional about date nights because we just love being with our kids so much. It is important to have dates out alone though. I used to get invites from friends to go out to a movie, dinner, or a cooking party they are hosting after all of our kids go to bed. I have stopped saying yes because, honestly, I really don't enjoy being out with others, especially when I could be at home with my husband and kids. There are exceptions to this; however, most of the time, I prefer staying in with my family in the evenings.

The other boundary I try to make sure I set is giving myself time for self-care. I have realized, especially working in the counseling field, that if I don't take care of myself, then I really am in no shape to help others. Self-care is different for everyone. Some people enjoy reading books, writing, or watching movies. Others might enjoy getting pampered or taking the time to walk alone in Target or the grocery store. Whatever you choose, make sure it is something that recharges your battery and allows you to feel more alive than you did before.

Gentle ways to set healthy boundaries:

Name your limits: Be clear with others about what you feel comfortable doing. Do not feel that you have to compromise your time. Let others know where your top priorities lie.

Be assertive: Show others you are confident in your decisions by being direct with them but not rude.

Be self-aware: When you are aware of your emotions and reactions to others, it helps you gauge your ability to help others. Make self-care a priority so that you are fully equipped to be there for other people.

Give yourself permission: Remember, you are responsible for yourself and how much you commit yourself to. Give yourself permission to set healthy boundaries with others, including family.

CHAPTER FOUR

Back to the Basics

I often ask my clients to list five different emotions off of the top of their head. I usually get responses such as sad, mad, and happy. Rarely does it go any deeper than that. Here's the deal: We are emotional beings. We were created to feel a wide range of feelings. For example, imagine a toddler kicking and screaming while throwing a temper tantrum. The types of phrases a parent might say to this screaming toddler include "Knock it off," "Quit crying," "Big girls don't cry," or even the dreaded "Act like a man." Toddlers and young children were not born with the ability to know how to express themselves. Small children should be taught that when they are screaming and acting up, the feeling they might have is that of anger. Instead, generation after generation, children seem to lack the basic skills of identifying emotions. This social deficiency has led to individuals learning to cope through anxiety, depression, cutting themselves, substance abuse, and anger.

It is important that girls and boys learn how to understand what emotions are. They need to learn how to express them in a healthy manner, starting at an early age. If we can get our children to express themselves in this way, their childhood will be calmer and your job as parents will (theoretically) be easier. This is another reason why so many parents of young children are now leaning toward teaching their kids sign language before they are able to speak. Teaching kids to communicate at an early age helps kids feel more in control of their emotions. It also makes them feel heard and understood.

We experience a wide range of both positive and negative feelings on a daily basis. Often times, we become people who internalize our feelings because we were not taught how to regulate our emotions. We end up becoming a person we were not meant to be. I personally have to work on this concept with my own kids a lot. I can get frustrated and lose my temper over the smallest of things. In doing this, I ask myself if I am helping my kids grow and develop into human beings who will be fully integrated into society once they are adults, or if I am enabling them to have entitled attitudes. I have been trying to be intentional with my kids, using those tough moments as a lesson instead of getting upset, yelling, and shutting down. This isn't always easy. I definitely have my moments when I fail and the neighbors can probably hear me during those moments. I have my moments when all four kids are pulling me in different directions and talking over each other all at once. I have my moments when I am overwhelmed, and it's okay. I just "do the next right thing." Breaking things down into steps instead of looking at the big picture can help you move forward instead of getting stuck in an ugly pattern of defeat.

In fact, this has become a common motto in my daily life. Every time I become overwhelmed with daily chores, homework meltdowns, piles of laundry, and paperwork, I can take a deep breath and remind myself to live in the moment and just do the next right thing.

> *Teaching kids to communicate at an early age helps kids feel more in control of their emotions. It also makes them feel heard and understood.*

Figure 1. A Feeling Wheel, which can be used to teach fundamental skills in identifying a person's emotion.

When it comes to emotions, one way I like to try to break things down into smaller steps is through the use of a Feeling Wheel. I love the Feeling Wheel exercise. See Figure 1. While there are a lot of different ways to use this wheel, I am going to tell you how I like to use it as an exercise to teach a basic understanding of emotions. I use this exercise a lot in my practice. It can seem a little childish at first, but a lot of my clients end up emailing me, asking for an electronic copy as well. I tell the person to pick one crayon. I then ask them to think of everything that has occurred from the moment they woke up until the present moment. They are then asked to color in a sliver of each emotion they have experienced that day. After a few minutes, we are able to process through each emotion and the event that led to that emotion. I have clients continue this process for a week at home, using the same feeling wheel but a different color for each day. We then come back the following session and process their emotions.

It's amazing how many people will say that they never realized how many emotions they can have in a given day and that they can experience both positive and negative feelings in such a short amount of time. When this exercise is done for an entire week, the results are amazing. Your brain will start to automatically recognize the feelings you feel in a given moment, which will help you process experiences throughout your day as each instance happens instead of letting it build up.

Sometimes living in the moment is the best gift you can give yourself.

I was once in the emergency room with a family member, and I'm sure if you have ever been in the ER, you know how hectic it can get. Of course, we were there for hours, because it's never a fast visit, and I started to get a little on edge. I was starving, and there were a lot of other things going on as well. A couple curtains over was a mother who was a patient, and she had her little girl with her. Her daughter couldn't have been much older than five years old and had a baby doll that cried every so often. If only the cry was a soft, sweet cry, but it wasn't. This baby doll would wail every couple of minutes. It was so loud and annoying. I found myself becoming a little irritated, so I took a step back and tried to put myself in that five-year-old little girl's shoes.

Here she was alone with her mother, who was laying in a hospital bed with an intravenous (IV) drip stuck in her arm. What a scary situation for a young girl! I quickly realized that she was comforted by making her baby doll cry and being able to make the crying stop. This was a projection of how much she wished she could comfort her mother, but she didn't know how. That baby doll was that little girl's comfort in a scary moment. I felt like such a horrible person after that, but I'm also glad I was able to step into her shoes to see what was really going on with her emotions. She did a great job regulating those emotions.

Sometimes living in the moment is the best gift you can give yourself. Being able to write and having my little girl climb into my lap with her baby doll, I know these moments won't last forever, and I am thankful for every time I've been able to take a break and cuddle for a few minutes. With today's constant hustle and bustle, it can be hard to stop for a second. Think about how much better you will feel when you allow yourself the extra time to just be present in the moment. Maybe then you will see something you have never realized before. I know I added a little something extra to my daughter's day every time I held her and showed her how much she is loved. It gives me peace. It gives her peace.

In treatment, all of the negative things I did were stripped away and I had to start processing my feelings.1

Demi Lovato

CHAPTER FIVE

Trials

Not every day will be the perfect opportunity to stop and live in the moment. However, I hope you can make more time for these moments because they can be life-changing. There are a lot of hard things we all go through. John 16:33 says, "I have told you these things, so that in me you may have peace. In this world you will have trouble. But take heart! I have overcome the world."[1] When I became a believer in Christ, I was coming out of a time of trials. I thought I would have peace and not have to endure more struggles than I already had. I was so wrong. Becoming a Christian means the opposite. We will be met with trials and struggles, and we will be tested. If we have God in our corner, cheering us on, and know that in the end, His plan is perfect, then we will have that peace one day, when we are called home. In the meantime, we will all have struggles from time to time. You

What I want you to know is that you will be okay, and you are making the best decision you can for yourself right now.

might be a new mother drowning in the everyday struggle of caring for a newborn while also feeling the pressure to have to be a good wife and housekeeper. You might be feeling guilty because you haven't made your son's last eight baseball games due to work. You might be the person who hides in your home because your anxiety and depression are beyond crippling. What I want you to know is that you will be okay, and you are making the best decision you can for yourself right now. All that matters to your family is that you are present when you are around them.

I had a client who was physically abused for years by her husband. She had two children and has since decided to leave him and pursue a divorce. She became overly depressed and slipped into a hard time when all she wanted to do was sleep and stay at home. Although she felt awful, she still made every one of her sessions. During one of these sessions, she was expressing how guilty she felt that she didn't do more with her kids. She didn't have the energy or the financial stability to do anything extra.

One day, she was lying in her bed, reading a book, and one of her sons came in to lay with her and talk. It was at that moment that she realized she was there for him to be able to open up and talk about what was going on in his life. What would have happened if she were busy doing the other things she felt pressured to do? Would her son have come to her to talk or would he think his mother was too busy? Would he have let the opportunity pass? This mother learned the importance of being present, and her son learned that it's okay to feel sad, that even when his mother was struggling, she still cared enough to stop and listen.

I know we are all struggling with something right now. I know life can feel like it keeps throwing curve balls, and we wonder if it will get any easier. We wonder what is the purpose of these trying times. I don't have those answers, but I do know, through each one of my experiences, I was able to learn a little more about myself, my life, and who I was meant to be.

One of the hardest times in my life since being a teenager came just before my fourth child was born. I had already had three children, and my youngest was six months old when I found out we were expecting again. This was not in our plan but also not something we were upset about. Children are a gift, and we love each of ours, in all of their uniqueness. I have to admit, I was definitely nervous about being a mother to four children, two of whom would be in diapers at the same time, and also managing a private practice and many other things. I started to settle into the idea of all the love and chaos that was about to unfold when I was hit by yet another boulder. At my 20-week ultrasound check, my doctor realized my baby girl wasn't growing properly. I was referred to a high-risk doctor's office, where I was then monitored every other week to assess for any positive or negative changes. This was hard enough as it was because I had two kids in school and a young one at home with me most days.

When I was 37 weeks pregnant, I went in for another routine checkup with the high-risk doctor. It was at this point the doctor realized my baby girl had stopped growing around the 32-week mark. The doctor told me to immediately head up to labor and delivery so that I could be induced. But of course, I wasn't ready, and I left, refusing the medical advice of my high-risk doctor. You see, I thought I was in control, but God quickly showed me I most certainly was not. He was, and is, and will always be.

I ended up having to be induced a couple of days later. I went through one of the worst birth experiences I had had yet. My baby girl's heart rate dropped, and because the umbilical cord was wrapped around her tiny body, with each contraction, the cord was pulling her back up the canal instead of lowering her into the birthing position. Of course, we didn't know the extent of the situation at the time, but at some point all I remember is the doctor yelling,

"C-section, stat." I remember looking up and seeing the bright lights and thinking of Grey's Anatomy as I was wheeled down the hall to the delivery surgical room. I was terrified. Tears rolled down my cheeks as the unknown approached me. A few minutes later, my husband was by my side and my baby girl was delivered. I eventually heard her cry and I thought the hard part was over. My baby girl weighed in at just 3 pounds and 13 ounces. She spent a week in the NICU but was otherwise perfect. I later found out that had she been delivered naturally, she most likely wouldn't have made it. What a whirlwind of emotions.

I am beyond thankful she is thriving and we both made it past that day. I still don't understand God's purpose in the unexpected and hard pregnancy or the traumatic birth experience, but I don't have to. What I did learn is that I don't have the control that I so desperately seek and think I do. I had to trust and believe in every part of His plan for me and this baby.

It didn't stop there either. After the birth, I was faced with having to take time off from the private practice that I had built up. It didn't make sense to put two young kids in daycare, especially with one of them being so little. The money just didn't add up at the time, so taking some time off from work to focus on being a mommy to these four wonderful children seemed like the right decision. In my heart of hearts, I believe God knew my desire to want to be home with my kids when they are young, and while I wasn't able to be home with the first two, I was given the opportunity to be home with the second two.

It was also during this time when I realized who the genuine people in my life were. Ever heard the saying "it takes a village to raise a child"? I have four children, and I'm not sure even a village will cut it, more like a small city! I have had so many friends enter my life who I thought were good-hearted people, who genuinely cared about me and my family. This couldn't have been further from the truth. Having always been a bit too trusting, I allowed others to enter my and my family's lives but quickly realized how toxic these relationships were.

I have had my fair share of toxic relationships, and oftentimes, cutting these relationships off has led to having feelings of rejection for me. Rejection can be hard to deal with. Maybe you know someone who was disowned by friends and family because they came out as homosexual, or maybe you know someone who became pregnant out of wedlock. It doesn't even have to be that intense. I know people who have felt rejected by friends because they had a different perspective than those friends. Sadly, a lot of people can probably relate to these feelings.

We were all born sinners, and by the grace of God, we have been saved, but that also means we are not perfect and may unintentionally hurt someone close to us. When things were a little hard for me over the last couple of years, I lost a couple of friends. It felt like pure rejection. I wondered if they didn't want to be around me. I wondered if I did something or said something that was offensive. I started to really dislike people, and that's definitely not good as a mental health counselor. I started to feel that people only looked out for themselves, and that's when I really started to guard my heart more. After the birth of my last child, I started to see who my truly genuine friends and family were. You know that one friend that stays with you overnight in the hospital and helps you hold back your hair while you vomit after having a baby? That friend who gives your baby her first bath in NICU because you were hurting so much while recovering from your C-section? I found that one friend, and she is my person and I will always be her person as well.

After her, I started to slowly find "my tribe," the people who stick by me through thick and thin and would mother my children should I need them to at any moment. It's important to be connected and find the people in your life who you can rely on for support and encouragement. It's also important for you to be that person to someone else. We are not meant to be alone in this life. We were made to love others and be intentional in our actions. So I ask you… who is in your tribe?

Helpful ways to deal with rejection:

Acknowledge your emotions: It's always best to work through your feelings in every situation. When you suppress your feelings, you are allowing yourself to harbor resentment toward others. This will only hold you back from true forgiveness.

Don't let rejection define you: Refuse to allow the perception of rejection to define who you are. Instead, try to understand that when you feel rejected in a situation or by someone else, it is usually the other person's own insecurities behind the act. Remember that other people's opinions are just that, their opinions. They hold no weight on who you are as a person.

Move on: Don't entertain relationships that are a one-way street. Find others to allow into your life who will lift you up in a positive way. Surround yourself with others who will show genuine care for you and help you continue to define your own identity. Find your tribe. Find your village. They are out there somewhere.

CHAPTER SIX

Being Intentional

You would think, after four kids, I would have realized I really don't have control over much. I mean, when I became a mom, I thought every day would be magical. I thought my kids would always listen to me and play nicely and quietly.... That was a joke. I can remember times when my older kids were riding their scooters in the house, and my two younger ones were trying to find objects to climb on. What I have learned, though, is each child is different, requires different needs, and thrives in an environment where others are intentional in their actions with them. And being intentional isn't just for children either, but for everyone in our lives.

So often we are distracted by our electronics, so our attention is divided. This goes for being in social groups as well. I can't tell you how many times we have gone out to dinner and looked around to see everyone on their phone instead of paying attention to those around them. I have come to love the idea of phone-free dinners, the kind where everyone places their phone or electronics in a bucket, and whoever touches theirs first during dinner gets stuck with the bill. Would you be paying for everyone's dinner or would you be relaxed because you know your dinner is about to be paid for? I often wonder if this contributes to the reason a lot of people love seeing a counselor—well, once they get past the stigma and realize they aren't crazy or weak. When you are in session with a counselor, the counselor is 100 percent present with you (or at least they are supposed to be). It feels good to have someone's undivided attention.

Being intentional in everything you do means you are taking the time to do things with a purpose in your daily words and your daily actions. When we take the time to slow down and focus on what is in front of us, we are prioritizing our lives.

I love that even as I was writing different chapters in this book, God allowed me to experience what I'm writing about. One instance, as I wrote outside with my two oldest girls, the weather was absolutely beautiful. It was about 67 degrees, windy, and I could feel the warmth of the sun beating down on my face. (I love this kind of weather because it's not that often we get it in the sunshine state.

We should be intentional in our dreams and aspirations.

It's usually so hot that walking to your mailbox ends up with yourself drenched with sweat.) My toddler caught my eye, ran up to me, and jumped in my arms. I was on a roll, typing about being intentional, so I decided to do just that. We lay in the grass together and named the different animals we could hear. We talked about God's creation on that beautiful day. I wouldn't have wanted to miss that moment for anything, even if it meant losing my train of thought in my writing.

As I think about being intentional, I remember a comment a friend once made, and it completely blows my mind what she believes it means to be intentional with others. I loved that her word for the year was intention. She explained that in everything she did and said, she asked herself the simple question: What is my intention?

She gave a great example of cooking dinner for her family. She explained that she decided to cook meals for her family because her intent was to bring her family closer and have stronger bonds by sitting around the family dinner table together. She also gave another example of when she was able to turn this question around. If at any point she felt hurt by another person's words, she would ask the person to clarify what they meant by asking them what their intention was behind the conversation. This allowed both parties to better understand each other's perceptions. How amazing is this! Being intentional can mean so many things to different people, but in all ways, it is meant to make us better people for ourselves, our family, and our friends.

It's great to be intentional when it comes to being with others, but there is also another way to be intentional in life. We should be intentional in our dreams and aspirations. It can be so easy to allow the days to pass us by and not get a lot done. While I fully believe in mental health days when you just do nothing, I also believe we were designed to contribute to this world.

We need to be intentional about our days. I love having a digital calendar where I can map out the things I know are important for me to accomplish in a given day. My husband, on the other hand, still writes out his agenda and "to-dos" for each day in a notebook he carries with him. To each their own. Having a plan helps keep us on track and motivated to accomplish our goals. Have you ever set a goal and then, months later, wondered why it wasn't ever accomplished? Let's look at New Year's resolutions as an example. A lot of resolutions are about people wanting to lose weight. While making a goal is important, the follow through, being intentional in doing the things necessary to lose weight, is also of equal importance. Mapping out the days and times you set aside to work out or logging your meals each day are great ways to stay intentional and on track with meeting your goals.

I personally do not do New Year's resolutions anymore. I would usually decide one month that I want to accomplish something, like write another book, and I set time aside to do just that despite the million other things I have going on as well. Do you have a goal you want to see come true? And if so, what are the steps you are willing to take to set those goals in motion?

I was talking to a friend about how she really would like to take a full year to get herself back on track, both mentally and physically. She stated she really needed to find a primary care doctor and a pediatrician for her kids because she had made a recent move to a new city. Fast forward a couple of months when I called her to talk. She again mentioned to me about needing to find these physicians. You see, she had a goal but did have the steps intentionally written out to achieve these goals. Time quickly passed her by, and months later, she was no closer to finding the doctors she needed for herself and her kids.

You are constantly changing and evolving, and so are your aspirations.

I remember saying to her that I also needed to make an appointment I had also been putting off. We made an agreement right then to hold each other accountable. We gave each other until the end of the day to meet our goals. When we checked back in with each other at the end of the day, we both were pleased to hear that we had met our goals for that day. Something so simple, yet was taking months to accomplish, was done in just a couple of hours due to being held accountable and staying within a community.

Another great idea for accountability is creating a vision board. It's a board you create to display your personal dreams and goals so that it is visible enough to help hold you accountable in achieving them. Of course, your vision board will change with time, and that's the awesome part! You are constantly changing and evolving, and

42

so are your aspirations. Personally, I would love a board that has a black, matte background (my favorite color is black, so it's inspiring to me). I would have pictures of a house in the mountains, a Disney cruise, an image of me enjoying public speaking (because I most definitely do not now), a picture of Christmas time in the snow, and maybe a bottle of wine. What about you?

Vision boards are great for those of us who have a type A personality. We tend to be (according to Google) very organized, outgoing, ambitious, sensitive, anxious, proactive, and concerned with time management. Does this sound at all like you? I know I definitely fit in the type A category. These traits are not necessarily a bad thing, because we can get a lot done. This also means we like to have things in our control. This is hard to do even when you are trying to be intentional because we can't control other people's behaviors or emotions.

I learned this lesson many times when it came to kids, especially my two-year-old. Wow, her emotions could be all over the place. One minute she loved me, and the next, she was screaming on the floor because I gave her the wrong colored sippy cup. One minute she was sweet, happy, and fun loving, and the next, demanding, whining and complaining. Most of the time, I never knew which side of my child I would get. A great example of this was when she jumped in my lap and hugged me, but then not even two seconds later, she threw herself off my lap and screamed she needed a band-aid for the "boo-boo" on her foot, which I saw no evidence of.

My older kids were this way too, just not as toddler-ish. Some days, I would wake up and be in a great mood, along with at least two or three of my kids. Almost always, one of them had to be in a bad mood, though. As much as I wished I could control them and make them more pleasant to be around, I have learned I can't.

Loving them intentionally also means loving them where they are. Wow, what a hard concept to even consider. The idea of loving people where they are in life can be so difficult for a lot of us, but the fact is, we can't change anyone.

I remember when I was just starting out as a counselor, and I would have a new client come in who was depressed. After talking with them for a while, I would get really excited because I could envision where they would be emotionally after a few sessions of counseling. In my mind, I wanted them to go from 0 to 100 percent feeling better because I knew they would enjoy life so much more. What I realized was that I wasn't helping them at all because I wasn't meeting them where they were at that moment. Sometimes, just sitting with them and listening is more important than jumping straight into the healing process.

We all come from different paths of life. If we can't love one another where we are in that walk, then being able to count on others just becomes a little more difficult. I was recently talking with another mom who was telling me a little about her life story, which is beautiful and inspiring and by all means, needs to be shared for others to hear and benefit from.

She shared with me how she came from a happy home until her parents decided to get a divorce. She stayed with her mother after believing her father had abandoned them. Her life started to spiral out of control when her mother became involved with drugs and alcohol and the wrong type of men. She experienced her first incident of sexual abuse when she was just six years old, by her cousin. For years, she was raised by her sister because her mother was often absent. For years, she didn't know when or where her next meal would come from. For years, she continued to experience trauma after trauma. How awful it must have felt for that six-year-old girl to learn some hard truths about life at such a young age.

I wonder how she felt when her mother and father intentionally checked out of her life.

As children, we should be able to count on the very people who brought us into this world or the people who decided to adopt us when our biological parents weren't able to care for us. It's a hard truth to face when we have to question the love of those who should be there for us every step of the way. Remember, being intentional means showing your unconditional love for others and placing their needs ahead of our own wants or desires.

Helpful ways to stay intentional:

Throw out indecisiveness: Be intentional in making decisions for yourself. Decide and map out how you want to live your life and what you want to include in your schedule. Decide who you want in your life and to what extent.

Practice self-care: You cannot be intentional with others if you are neglecting yourself. Preserve your energy for what matters most to you. Eat healthy, exercise daily, and give yourself a moment of peace each day.

Speak positive words: The way we speak to ourselves and others will either have a positive or negative impact. Speak positive and motivational words into existence. Doing this will help increase your confidence and resilience in life.

Show mindful gestures: Let others know you are fully present with them. Kiss your significant other, talk to your children about their day, give a friend a hug, laugh, live and dance!

CHAPTER SEVEN

Unconditional Love

I try to love each of my kids in the best way that fits their personalities. What might work for one child may not necessarily work for the other. I have one child who is very sensitive and loves spending quality time with me and the family. I try to do mini dates to show him how much he is loved. One of my other kids responds better to acts of kindness. She loves having other people do things for her. But even when I try to be intentional with my kids and their individual needs, I won't always get it right. What I want my children to grow up knowing is that they are and will always be loved unconditionally by me.

When we are intentional, we are loving people where they are in their journey. When we love unconditionally, we are loving someone for who they are. Unconditional love means to love someone without expecting anything from them for that love. Loving unconditionally means not placing conditions or limits for that love on anyone else. I feel like this is one of the hardest life lessons to accomplish, especially when the people we are trying to love unconditionally are not our flesh and blood.

Think of a brand new mama who is about to give birth to her firstborn. Before we become mothers, we think we have a good understanding of how much we will love that child, but in reality, we get hit with a variety of overwhelming emotions. The moment that baby is placed in your arms, whether it be a biological child or a child you chose to adopt into your family, your life and view of love are challenged in that instant. Life becomes about that new bundle of joy and not about you or anyone else anymore. You finally know what it feels like to want to give your own life if it means saving your child's life.

I know not all mamas feel this way instantly because of outside circumstances surrounding the pregnancy or other factors, so if you are struggling, I urge you to reach out. A lot of women, approximately 15 percent[1], will experience postpartum depression symptoms. Postpartum depression is a clinical depression and mood disorder that can occur after the birth of a baby. It is not to be confused with the baby blues. The baby blues are experienced by approximately 50-70 percent[2] of new mothers within the first week of the baby being born but disappear after a while. A couple mothers in one of my mother's groups described postpartum depression below (Initials were used in order to protect their privacy).

> *"I wanted an avalanche to fall on me to get away from the crying infant and needy dog. A no-fault deadly car accident would have also been welcome. I didn't want to commit suicide or otherwise harm myself or others, but a natural accident sounded like a convenient solution to end the awful feelings and exhaustion."* M.

> *"I never wanted to kill myself. I just felt like everything I did was stupid or a complete failure. I also felt like I didn't matter to anyone and made sure to make myself even more isolated and unavailable by not picking up phone calls from family/friends even though I really wanted them to visit me."* E.

"Postpartum Depression made me feel hopeless while I was holding hope. I felt darkness when there should have been light. My entire life changed and postpartum wouldn't let me adapt." A.

"I remember going to my OB a couple of months after my son was born saying the words he is better off without me. I am absolutely horrified by that memory. Never felt so alone." N.

I don't know about you, but when I read those words, I can almost feel the pain of the emotions these mamas were going through. It must have been so tough to struggle and be pulled into a world where all you can see is darkness, especially during a time when happiness and light should have shown through.

I have also been through a tough pregnancy and birth, and was diagnosed with post-traumatic stress disorder after the birth. I know what it feels like to sit and cry because your newborn is crying and needs you but you can't get up to comfort them. I know what it feels like to feel guilty over feeling this way. I also know what it feels like to come out of that experience and to instead experience the amazing feeling of unconditional love for that newborn. There is hope and help, mamas. You are not alone, and seeking help from a professional during this extremely vulnerable time is essential. Even I, being a licensed mental health counselor, had to have my own counselor to work through my struggle. Let me tell you, I also felt extreme guilt over being a professional myself and needing to seek outside help. I realized that I am just as human as anyone else. I desired to be able to seek help when I needed it most to make me a better person and mother.

We might go through difficult times when it seems hard to show love, but that is the beauty of unconditional love. It is a type of love that is ingrained in our being and can't be easily taken away.

In 1 John 3:18, it says, "Dear children, let us not love with words or speech but with actions and in truth."[3] This verse doesn't say to only show true love to those in your family, but rather show true love to everyone: your neighbors, your friends, even the person you just met a couple of minutes ago! This concept can be so hard for so many people to grasp, especially me.

I used to be so loving and trusting of pretty much everyone. I used to only see the good in people and would always try to give the benefit of the doubt. Then I was hit by some very hurtful relationships with friends, and I shut down. I stopped believing in the good in people and instead shifted toward isolation. I pulled myself away from these friends because of how badly they hurt me, and I felt bitter. After a while, however, I realized I wasn't allowing myself to love anyone unconditionally. Truth is, it doesn't matter if we get hurt by others as long as we can set healthy boundaries and decide to forgive. In forgiving, we are loving others unconditionally.

I also realized that loving other people is more difficult when we don't have a love for ourselves. Self-love is accepting who you are while working to improve the things you don't like. It is learning to accept the things you can't change. It is acknowledging the scariest parts of yourself and understanding your whole being. It is accepting the fact that you are human and, therefore, are not perfect. Self-love doesn't always come easy; we can be very critical of ourselves. You will make mistakes, but practice trying to be less hard on yourself. Become mindful of your needs over your wants and practice self-care. Learn to love yourself unconditionally, and you will become better equipped to love other people.

When I have asked others about what comes to mind when they hear the words "unconditional love," I have heard a lot of references to family pets. I know this probably seems a little humorous at first, but I guess when you really think about it, pets make great companions who are almost always faithful. They're "a man's best friend." You can tell your pet anything, and guess what? They can't repeat it! Well, unless they're a parrot. Not only that, a pet knows no stigma or cultural boundary. They don't care if you are black, white, yellow, green, thin, thick, or about your political preferences. Of course, pets are not for everyone, but I can understand the desire to be around an animal who shows unconditional love and affection over the guesswork of dealing with human love.

We, as humans, crave the love and acceptance of other people around us. We can do this almost to the point of compromising ourselves. As kids, we do not deviate too much from our fundamental teachings for fear our parents will not love us if we are different than they are. I think about how much this holds us back from realizing our dreams in life. It's amazing when we can finally break out of that shell of fear and be who we were meant to be. It would be amazing if we, as friends, could decide to love each other without conditions and build each other up to achieve our greatest potential. Of course, you should have standards and surround yourself with positive people, but we should think about loving people where they are in their lives.

Loving unconditionally does not always come naturally. I believe it is a conscious choice we have to make on a daily basis. I was recently in an argument with my husband. I felt he was shutting down and getting angry over something that was out of my control, so I started to question his unconditional love for me. I didn't question his love for me, but rather the feeling of him placing conditions on me to be able to want to express his love for me. We ended up talking it through and that's when I realized it's a choice.

A friend of mine from college was able to experience unconditional love in one of the most amazing ways. Throughout our undergraduate studies, we were inseparable. We called ourselves "partners in crime." After college, I moved back home, and he stayed in Jacksonville, Florida, for another year. It wasn't until he decided to move back to the same hometown over a year later that he realized he was homosexual. He knew at some point he would need to tell his parents, but it made him nervous at the time. He wondered if his parents would approve and wondered how they would react. He wondered if his parents would continue to love him.

He decided to tell his mother first. He was shocked when her reaction was relief. She ended up telling him she had her suspicions and was glad he finally confirmed them. She told him she loved him no matter who he was attracted to and only wanted him to eventually find someone to be with who made him happy.

After he told his mother, he had enough courage to talk with his father. His father assured him as well that no matter what, he would always love him. His main concerns were for his son to protect and take care of himself.

I can't imagine how that must have felt, to go from wondering if he would still be accepted and loved by his parents to his parents openly loving him with unconditional love. You see, his parents did not necessarily have to understand the choices he made or believe in them. What they did—and we should all learn from them—is accept and love him where he was. They made him feel confident, loved, and accepted.

This type of love isn't necessarily shared by everyone. There are people out there who are horrible people. There are people who choose to abuse their significant other or even choose to abuse their own children, whether that means emotionally, physically, sexually, or mentally. This is not unconditional love. This is not love at all. It is never okay to allow other people to treat you this way. You deserve better than this. You deserve to be adored. You deserve to not have to do or be anything in order to receive love from anyone.

Love is a choice. Love can be felt at different levels. If there is anything I want you to take away from this chapter, it is to remember that there are no limitations set in unconditional love. The people who will love you and appreciate you for who you are will be the people who will guard your heart with their heart. These are the people I will choose to keep close in my life. I encourage you to do the same.

Unconditional Love is our birthright, not judgement or condemnation, and there's nothing we need to do to earn it. This is simply who and what we are.[4]

Anita Moorjani

CHAPTER EIGHT

Control

I know you just read the title and thought, Yeah, I need some of that in my life. Don't we all? As I said before in a previous chapter, I crave being in control over everything in my life. When I don't have that control, I tend to experience a lot of anxiety, the kind where my heart starts to pound, tears start to pile in my eyes, and I get HOT! I know we can't always have control; God has really shown me that He is ultimately in control, and I am not. He has shown me areas where I need to let go of control.

Thunderstorms are a good example. I love thunderstorms! They are about the only time during the summer months that I absolutely love. The sun disappears, dark clouds roll in, the smell in the air becomes more intense, and then you hear the rumble. I love hearing thunder and seeing lightning crash through the clouds. I love that thunderstorms can be a little scary and unpredictable. I love how thunderstorms remind me that I am not always in control. They force you to stop what you are doing and enjoy the magic.

Being in control means having the power to influence others, direct their actions, and influence the course of events. I don't know about you, but I certainly don't have much control over such things. The only control we have is over ourselves. We cannot control other people's actions, opinions, or behaviors. We cannot control what others think of us. We cannot control anyone but ourselves. Of course, we can plan, but we also need to be prepared for the unexpected because we all know that not everything works out perfectly.

I liked testing my boundaries as a teenager. I can't think of anyone that age who doesn't. I constantly felt like my parents were trying to control me. I perceived them as trying to tame my individuality when I was in a time of exploring who I was as a person. We all know teenagers know everything, right? I mean, heck, my two-year-old seems to know everything already. I remember trying to control my self-image by battling anorexia, dying my hair, and smoking. I liked the thrill of the possibility of getting caught and seeing how my parents would react, knowing I was engaging in something they disapproved of. It sounds so stupid to me now, and I still feel bad about what I put my parents through. I just pray my kids don't choose to put me and my husband through it as well.

In fact, I have started implementing different strategies and techniques to allow my kids the opportunity to believe they have some control over their lives and their decisions. Kids not only crave independence and control, but they also tend to thrive in environments where there is structure and rules. I think it's so funny how outsiders will look at my girls on the days they decide they want to dress themselves. My grandma used to ask me why I would allow my girls to leave the house in unmatched outfits and with what she thought was "untidy" hair. I, on the other hand, love that my girls want to express their unique personalities and have a say in their outfits. I love that I am helping build their confidence in a world where so many girls lack a sense of self-worth.

I once read a book by Danny Silk called Loving Your Kids on Purpose, and it hit home with the way I wanted to parent my kids. He talks a lot about giving our kids choices in life. It never dawned on me that giving kids a choice in things around them would allow them to feel they have some control in their lives, and therefore, eliminate some—not all—of the urge to rebel in order to show independence.

A great example of this concept is when one of my friends decided her teenagers needed to go to youth group to meet more positive friends and adults. Her kids fought her on the idea and even asked her what the consequences would be if they decided not to go. I remember jokingly asking her if she had to physically pull them to the car to go to youth group if they refused. Her response was great. She calmly stated that she gave them two choices. The first choice was to attend youth group alone, or the second choice was to attend youth group with their mother so they wouldn't feel uncomfortable. Of course, they chose to go to youth group alone.

The point here is that this mother's end goal was to get her kids to attend youth group. She put the control in their hands by giving them a choice. She chose an option she knew they probably wouldn't take and an option they were more likely to take. She knew that, either way, her end goal was to get them to try youth group. In the end, they did and they enjoyed it. Even just the perception of control can change a person's attitude positively. Of course, you will have those kids who don't choose option A or B but instead C. Oh, I love those stubborn little ones. The choice is then up to the parents. "You choose or I choose."

Don't you just love it when you have a plan and think it's going to go great, and then all of a sudden, BAM! God laughs when we plan for our life because, ultimately, He knows the real plan and knows it probably won't turn out exactly how we think it will.

I had a teenage client who was adopted at a young age into a very loving family. She was raised by her adoptive parents and has one adoptive sibling. Like any teenager, she could be a little defiant toward her parents and get into some trouble. She also struggled with the fact that she did not know her biological mother or where she came from. One day, she disclosed to me that she had become sexually active with her boyfriend. After many conversations about safe sex, she eventually told her mother, who was very supportive. Her mother took her to get the birth control implantation in her arm. The day she received the implant, they also tested her for pregnancy, which to her relief came up negative.

A couple of weeks later, she found out she was indeed pregnant during the first test, but it had been too early to be detected. For months she thought the right choice was to place her baby for adoption. She planned to go back to her normal teenage life after the birth of her daughter. It wasn't until she had given birth and held her baby girl that she decided she wanted her forever. The unexpected happened to her, and it was the best unexpected she could have ever imagined.

Someone once said, "I believe everything happens for a reason. People change so that you can learn to let go, things go wrong so that you appreciate them when they're right, you believe lies so you eventually learn to trust no one but yourself, and sometimes things fall apart so better things can fall together."[1]

I love this quote. So many times we think we are getting the short end of the stick, but it turns out for the better in the end. It's so hard going through the journey sometimes, but if we don't trust the process, we won't be able to reap the beautiful rewards at the end. If we can't let go of a little control and brace ourselves for the unexpected, then our lives will be boring. I don't know about you, but I don't want to live a life knowing every twist and turn. I want to immerse myself in the chaos and joys of this life and learn to roll with the punches. Of course I want to have some control over my life, and in a lot of areas, I do. It's about learning those areas and allowing myself to figure out how things work best for me.

We may not be able to have control over others, and other people can really get on our nerves at times, but we do have control over our surroundings, who we choose to interact with, and how we respond to others. If you find yourself in a bad situation, you can choose to leave. If you find yourself surrounded by negative people, you can choose to seek out more positive influences instead and/ or leave the situation altogether. Yes, this includes family members as well. It is better to surround yourself with positive influences so that you are lifted up and not dragged down. If you find yourself lying on the floor, crying and feeling like you can't breathe, get up, get moving, and know you will be okay, even if it isn't right away.

Life is meant to be lived fully. I believe we only get one shot at this life, and we can't let obstacles stand in our way. It's okay to fall, but get up again because you have control over your drive and how you choose to keep going or not.

An area I have found myself trying to control at times is the perception that other people have of me. I lose so much energy in trying to be the person other people want me to be in order to be happy and feel accepted. The problem is that the amount of energy it takes drains me, and then I have no time for the people or things in my life that really matter. It's funny because my husband always points out how I act or talk so differently when I am around my parents. I didn't really notice until I was on the phone with my mother one day, and my husband was in front of me. I noticed I was talking very "surface level," and after I got off the phone, my husband made the comment of how weird the conversation was that I just had. What was I afraid of?

I was afraid because I knew that I talked and acted differently when I was around my husband than when I was around my mother, and now he noticed it. But why did this frighten me? I now know that I allowed this to control the way in which I showed up when interacting with my mom. We can't always please everyone in our life, and we definitely are not going to be able to, so please take your control back and just focus on being the best version of yourself.

So often, even if it's on a subconscious level, we compare ourselves to others. This can be the death of us, or at least the death of moving forward in a positive way. How do you feel about social media? It can be awesome, but it can also be depressing. I have talked about the Pinterest perfect ideal images, and other social media platforms are no different. No one wants to share a picture of their life when it looks messy. How would others perceive you if you showed a picture of your house in disarray or a picture of you crying because of the fight you just got into with your husband or kids?

I once heard Karl Lagerfeld's saying: Personality begins where comparison ends.[2] I love this saying. When we compare ourselves, our lives, or our families to anything else, we are taking away our uniqueness. We are conforming and that is boring and stressful. We are also not being truthful to others because we are projecting an image that is not our own. I think of all those social media accounts that make the person's life seem amazing! No one's life is amazing all of the time, and when we constantly subject ourselves to this type of "perfection," we limit our joy. So maybe it's time for a social media break.

We think we need to run a perfect house, look a certain way, act a certain way and "fit in" with society's ideals and norms. We compare ourselves to each other and adjust our way of doing things to make sure we are accepted by others. Truth is, what works for me may not necessarily work for you, and that is okay. We need to stop comparing ourselves and our lives. Stop trying to keep up

with the girl next door. Stop trying to impress others around you.
Be fulfilled in yourself and choose to be happy.

You have the control to change your life.

Things you cannot control

The weather

Other people

What other people think

Your past

Things we can control

Your own actions

Your emotions

Your behavior

How you react to others

How you interpret situations

You have the control to change your life

CHAPTER NINE

Lowering the Bar

There have been many times I have felt that I had to live up to other people's expectations. If I didn't have a certain look or I didn't act a certain way, I thought I would be looked down upon. There was also the pressure of having expectations of other people. So many women long for their significant other to help them around the house. For the love, man, can you just do the dishes for once? Then they turn around and get upset when their partner loads the dishwasher in a completely different way than they would have. We tend to have high expectations of others, and most of the time, we don't realize it. It can become annoying when we are on the other end of those expectations.

Expectations are mostly seen in relationships with other people. Without relationships, we would not have the need to expect anything from other people or allow other people to expect anything from us. While it is essential to have close relationships with others, it is also important to check ourselves and the pressure we are putting on others or allowing others to put onto us. Unrealistic expectations will get in the way of our relationships. It is wonderful to have friendships, but it's equally as important to limit the time with others if and when needed.

Sometimes, this can also mean that you need to limit time with family, especially after the holiday season. Holidays can be fun, but they can also be very stressful because there are so many people in one area and each person has their own personality. Not every personality clicks and not every perspective is the same. This can be a recipe for disaster, especially when intertwining two families through marriage.

I have often felt both my husband and father expected a lot out of their relationship with each other. Each desired something different, and when they didn't find what they were looking for, they immediately became defensive and guarded. My dad grew up without a present father in his life. His father was an alcoholic and was not the best family man. My father, having only had daughters, later longed for a father-son relationship that he thought he could get from one of his sons-in-law.

My husband also grew up with an absent, alcoholic father. He felt the pressure to have to grow up and be the man of the house. He, in a sense, also became a father figure to his younger sister. He grew up only knowing that others relied on him. By the time we were married, my husband was not in search of a daddy figure. This cocktail of childhood experiences and the different methods of coping only led to hurt from both my husband and father. They were each expecting something different from the other person but never received the validation they both sought.

I believe they set their expectations of each other so high that when those expectations were not fulfilled, it only resulted in the perception of *Not every personality clicks and not every perspective is the same.* rejection. What would happen if they lowered their expectations of each other and instead chose to love one another for who they are and where they are in their lives? The end results could be beyond amazing! Going into a situation where you do not expect anything from someone means you will only be surprised when they exceed your lowered expectations. This also saves you from disappointment. It's hard to be disappointed in someone when you never expected anything of them in the first place.

I truly believe, at our core, we desire to be happy—happy with our lives and happy with ourselves. To an extent, happiness is a choice. When we have high expectations of other people and ourselves, we are robbing ourselves of happiness.

The key is to filter. Protect yourself from these people, whose only goal is to bring you down or rejoice in your struggles.

As stated in previous chapters, we do not have control over others. The only real control we have is over ourselves. People will let us down time and time again, so why not lower our expectations of others? When they exceed those expectations, we can be surprised and rejoice in those moments. Stop placing these standards on your family and friends! They don't need the extra pressure of having to try to please you. Life is hard enough.

I used to think that having many friends and/or acquaintances was a mission to strive for. When you have a lot of friends, it must mean people really like you, right? When I was in college and Facebook was big, it was awesome to have hundreds, if not thousands, of friends on your page. As I became a little older and wiser, I realized that having those few close friends is a lot more rewarding and intimate.

Many people will come in and out of our lives. You don't have to befriend all of them. Boundaries, my friend! There will be people who tear you down and want to eat you for lunch. There will be people who want to use and abuse you. There will be people who pretend to be your friend and then turn their backs on you the first chance they get. The key is to filter. Protect yourself from these people, whose only goal is to bring you down or rejoice in your struggles. They are not your true friends.

But don't forget to be nice and courteous to everyone you meet. Show them the love and respect you want in return. With each person that enters your life, evaluate the value of the potential friendship. Ask yourself, will this person help me to be the best person I can be by being a positive influence in my life? Make sure the friendship allows you to lift each other up, not pull each other down by one or the other expecting too much. The friendship needs to be beneficial to both of you. I'm not talking about giving and taking from each other. I am talking about an authentic friendship in which being around each other isn't about entertaining each other. It's about living life and walking through life with one another without judgment. Those, my friends, should be the expectations of allowing people into your life.

> *Everything in your life worth accomplishing is going to be hard work. Work hard, put your all into your goals, and move forward.*

I don't want you to confuse the idea of lowering your expectations with lowering your goals and dreams. Of course you should dream big and reach for the stars. When I talk about lowering your expectations, I mean that you shouldn't limit yourself. It's easy to have a major dream and goal in mind but how attainable is your dream if all you can see in front of you is the big picture? Lower your expectations. Reach for the stars and your big dream but do not try to jump from A to Z. Take your time to ensure you are taking the right steps, and when you fall, get back up and try it again. Start by doing small achievable steps. By doing this, you will later exceed your expectations and feel amazingly accomplished.

The idea of lowering your expectations of yourself is in itself an act of self-love. Over 300 million people experience depression worldwide and 50 percent of the people diagnosed with depression also experience anxiety.[1] I believe the idea of setting too high of expectations on yourself can be part of the problem. We can become sad, depressed, and/or anxious because when we do not attain the highest of our expectations, we feel we have failed ourselves. We are our biggest critics. We need to take a step back, take a breath, and strive to achieve what we can at that point in time. When you start to feel yourself slipping, that's a red flag and an indication that it is time to take care of yourself.

You can lower expectations but set high standards for yourself. Not everything needs to be "perfect." You know your limitations and you know your desires. Everything in your life worth accomplishing is going to be hard work. Work hard, put your all into your goals, and move forward. You've got this. Don't let anyone or anything stand in your way. Just because the world may tell you no or set different societal expectations on you, it does not mean you will fail if you choose to deviate from those ideals. Be an individual; be who you are and not who the world wants you to be. We will never be able to live up to the standards of the world, but we can live up to the standards we set for ourselves. It's your life to live and no one else can choose the way you live it.

I encourage you to figure out what works best for you, your family, your career, and your goals. What works for one person may not be the right fit for another person. And if you find yourself stressed and overwhelmed, change direction.

I have always heard that eating meals together as a family is beneficial in keeping a close connection. My family usually sat down at the table most nights, and my husband and I engaged with our kids. I, for one, didn't like the television to be on either, because of the distraction it creates for our kids. However, I knew another family that preferred to eat in front of the television as a family. Their perspective was different than ours in the fact that they had teenagers. The only way to get them to interact with their parents was when they sat as a family and watched shows during dinner. The mother best described it as keeping the family in one place long enough to interact positively during commercials.

I can't compare my family dinnertime to theirs because what worked great for them as a family with teenagers didn't work for us as a family with young children.

Stop comparing yourselves to other people and other families. When we compare, we kill our own happiness and set ourselves up for failure.

How to let go of unrealistic expectations:

Know your expectations: Try keeping a weekly or daily list of what your realistic expectations are. Write down any unrealistic expectations that you are placing on yourself and move them to a different day. Be flexible and set boundaries with yourself and others.

Evaluate your expectations: Have expectations of yourself and others only if they are not going to harm you in a negative way. Make sure the expectations you have helps you grow toward success.

Have compassion: Your expectations of others, even when low-ered, can at times cause disappointment when they are not upheld. Acknowledge your feelings and determine if the situation needs to be addressed or if you need to let it go.

CHAPTER TEN

Unclutter Your Life

I tried for a couple of years to only have one social media account....
okay, maybe two. I tried to limit myself in this area to create more
room for happiness and less comparison in my life. Then I realized
I could use social media to show the true nature of daily life, struggles and all. I'll have to admit, I didn't get an Instagram account
until later in the game and I didn't understand the hashtag thing
right away. But, wow, it can be powerful!

It took me a while to decide on a name but I finally decided
to name my Instagram account, @perfectlycluttered. My friend
helped me set it up and told me to put the @ sign in front of the
name (I'm still not 100 percent sure why). Anyway, I love the
name because it's an oxymoron. You can't be perfect, especially
in the area of clutter. No one's life is free of clutter either, but it
can be more manageable, hence the saying "perfectly cluttered"!

I love sharing images of disaster—like the ones that unfold in
the playroom, because we all know when you have kids, nothing
stays clean for too long, especially the playroom. I love showing
pictures of a family room that looks pretty tidy, but when you look
closely, there is a mound of clean, unfolded laundry in the corner.
The point of it all is that my life and my house is, to an extent,

"cluttered." It will eventually get done, but for now, I don't have to do it all and neither do you.

One lesson I have learned is to delegate. The most successful people have a community in which they rely on others to help them get things done. Delegating will help you prevent burnout and fatigue. I believe the key in delegating to others is first figuring out what your priorities are in life. My first priority is my kids. They mean the world to me. I chose to have these precious little ones, so my priority is making sure their needs are met while I teach them to be tiny humans who will eventually grow up to be successful. Let me tell you, it's not that easy. I can't be it all and do it all. I wish I could tell you that I'm superhuman and have the strength to work, clean, meal prep, workout, attend extra-curricular activities, and more, but the truth is, I am only one person. While I am capable of doing most of that, I am not capable of doing them every day and all at the same time, so I delegate.

Anything and everything you can find that will help make your life easier, you should be open to trying.

We have a cleaning company come into our home once a month to help with the deeper cleaning, and as a family, we pick an hour each weekend to spot clean together. I work part-time as a mental health counselor and the other days, I am home with my little ones. Oh, and I am the worst cook! I loathe cooking but will do it to feed my family when I have to. My hubby, on the other hand, has a knack for gourmet-style cooking. Almost every Sunday, he is in the kitchen making some masterpiece that will last us the entire week, and it is so yummy.

I encourage you to consider delegating if you are able to. I have heard of laundry services, meal prep companies, professional organizers, nannies, and so much more. By allowing other people to help you, you have removed some unnecessary clutter and have freed your mind for more substantial things. Anything and everything you can find that will help make your life easier, you should be open to trying.

I am definitely not by any means telling you that you need to have a clean home and that everything should be put in its place. What I want to tell you is that when you feel good about your environment and you are not overworked, then your physical, mental, and emotional health will sharpen. You will have more time to yourself. You will have the time to engage in personal growth and time for the things that really matter. You will become a more rounded person.

I speak to many of my younger clients' mothers, and they are so overwhelmed. They tell me they can't understand why their child is acting out and not doing well in school anymore. They tell me all of the sports and extra activities they have their kids involved in—martial arts, baseball, dance, soccer, drama club, gymnastics and the activities are almost every single night of the week. You would wonder how these children even have the time to act out.

Well, their life is too cluttered. And I know what you are thinking. How can a nine, ten, eleven year old's life be too cluttered? They are just kids for goodness sake. That's just it. They are just kids. While it is wonderful to have your children involved in a sport or hobby, it can also be overwhelming when they are overloaded. They need time to *There is no room in your life for people and things that are not going to lift you up in a positive way.* be children. They need time to run, play, and use their imaginations. By allowing this much clutter into their lives, we are, in a sense, teaching them to stay busy all of the time and not enjoy life in the moment. Sorry to break it to you, but this is not healthy.

I definitely believe kids should be active and be involved in something that helps bring them confidence. I also believe kids these days are not getting the tools they need to be able to create and be imaginative. For two Christmases, our kids received many outdoor toys, not the electric types either. We were once out all day long, playing in front of our house, and not once did we see any other children outside playing. Our neighborhood was filled with young kids! We later found out a lot of the kids in the neighborhood had received new video games for Christmas, and instead of running around outside, they were indoors. I'm not saying all video games are bad, but there does need to be a balance. We need to make sure our children's minds are not cluttered with unneeded things.

We can also unclutter our lives by removing unnecessary events and toxic people. There is no room in your life for people and things that are not going to lift you up in a positive way. Don't overload yourself with working, volunteering, watching your kids, watching your neighbors' kids, attending dinner parties, and saying yes to every invite that comes your way. I heard somewhere that if the answer isn't a "HELL YES, I want to do that," then the answer needs to be no.

Don't allow people into your life who will only bring you down and make you feel less than what and who you really are. We need to have friends in our lives that we can be real with and talk to about all of life's demands. Toxic people are like cancer. They will infect your lives with negative juice that will eventually rub off on you and your family. Get rid of them.... Unfriend, click.

Only allow yourself to keep things, people and events in your life and in your schedule if they bring you joy, inspire you, and give you purpose. Perfectly clutter your life with the things that will matter the most.

Children and adults will feel the effects of a packed life. It's important to simplify when you can. Here are a few tips and tricks from other mamas to help you simplify and unclutter your life.

"Making PBJ's for the week on Sunday and freezing them for easy lunch packing, buckets under the stairs for each kid to throw in whatever needs to go upstairs that night and be put away, freezing Go-GURTs (yogurts pops) and using them for desserts." L.

"I keep a basket in our pantry of easy grab and go snack foods —raisins, granola bars, pouches, gummy snacks, protein bars, prepackaged apricots, tiny containers with goldfish crackers. Then when we're running out the door or I'm packing a lunch it's just grab a few options and jet. We also keep socks in the shoe basket, or next to it. Helps to prevent having to run back down to the bedroom to get socks as we're trying to get out the door." M.

"The biggest improvement I made to my life was having set morning and evening routines——things we do every day no matter what. AM is empty dishwasher and start a load of laundry, on top of our getting ready busyness. PM is run dishwasher, cycle laundry, wipe counters, vacuum/mop. Each one takes about 20 minutes tops but keeps our house running so smoothly. Nothing really builds up because it is twice a day, proactive habit to take care of it. It took years to find a groove but it has changed our lives." L.

"We pick out school clothes for the week on Sunday night, so they can just Grab & Go in the morning." J.

"When crafting—mix glitter with Elmer's glue and let kids paint it with a paintbrush. No more glitter everywhere." B.

"Laundry basket in the laundry room for each kids' clean clothes. That way you don't have to always fold and put them away." L.

"Makeup in the car. Help the kids get ready in the morning and get your presentable face on in the car on the go." A.

CHAPTER ELEVEN

The Truth & Nothing but the Truth

Lying is a part of human nature. It can be a relationship separator, and it takes a certain measure of self-awareness to try to tell the truth as much as possible. Jan and Stan Berenstain once wrote: "No matter how you hope, no matter how you try, you can't make a truth out of a lie."[1]

In my field, when we are assessing a child who has disclosed that they have been touched inappropriately or were sexually abused, we first need to figure out if they know the difference between a lie and the truth. In order to find this out, we sit down and color with them. Coloring is often a childhood favorite. It takes pressure off of talking about the uncomfortable subject and allows for more kid-friendly, open dialogue. While coloring, we ask the child to name the different colors of crayons to be sure they know their colors. After we have established they know their colors, we then take a blue crayon for example, and we tell the child that the color is, say, pink. We then ask the child if that statement was a lie or the truth. Of course, the answer is that it is a lie. If they get it right, then we have established they most likely have a credible story and aren't confusing reality with make-believe.

I hate lying. I hate the idea of lying to anyone or anyone lying to me. It's just a nasty pet peeve of mine. I guess I feel like it speaks to a person's character, and I want to have higher standards for myself. I'm not talking about little white lies or hiding something for the good of another person, like when we tell our children that Santa Claus or the Tooth Fairy is real.

I do remember as a kid, though, learning that if I lied about something I did, there was a possibility of not getting into trouble. There was also a possibility of getting caught in a lie and getting double the punishment. Anyway, I tell you this because there seems to be greater benefits in telling the truth. Not just greater benefits because it is the right path to choose but because it makes you a credible person. It gives you integrity, speaks volumes to your character/moral compass, and allows others to trust you. It also allows others to feel you are a safe place for them.

I also remember, as a teenager, saying to my mother, "If you really don't want to know the answer to your question, then you probably shouldn't ask." I laugh now at the thought of this, but it's also kind of true. I had gotten to the point where I didn't want to lie anymore, so I gave my parents the choice to decide if they really wanted to know or not.

James E. Faust once said, "Honesty is more than not lying. It is truth telling, truth speaking, truth living and truth loving."[2] Speaking truth into your life and the lives of others creates a positive environment. It's being intentional in your conversations and being passionate for what you believe in. Of course, there are gray areas in the truth. People will omit or withhold information for the protection of others. While it may be the right choice at that moment, it can still be hurtful on the receiving end. I believe communication is an important component in guarding other people's hearts. Before I speak with someone, I try to ask myself if what I am about to tell them will hurt them or help them in some way. Sometimes, it seems I haven't made the right decision when the other person is upset, not necessarily with me but with the content of the conversation. I try to stand firm in knowing my intentions were good.

When you think about the idea of being truthful, I hope you also consider being truthful to yourself. So many times we try to be someone we are not and do things that do not fit with who we are. This is not being truthful to ourselves. This can and will eventually create burnout. I don't know about you but I can't always have my "game" face on. I know I need time to be alone and time to process things. Being true to yourself is showing others your authenticity. It's realizing your greatest, deepest needs and allowing yourself to embrace them.

Being true to yourself helps you build the confidence you need to develop your own identity. It's important to develop your own set of beliefs and stand up for those beliefs when they are confronted. No matter how young or old you are, or how small you may feel in this world, you need to know you have a voice. You are important. Realize you have the power to make your life what you want it to be. Align yourself with people that will encourage you. Don't let a simple setback stop you from moving forward.

When my mother was in college, she was studying to become a nurse, not necessarily because she desired to be a nurse—she hated the sight of blood—but because she knew it was her calling. Of course, she had other ambitions, but she felt this longing in her spirit and kept coming back to the idea of nursing school. She felt a better peace taking this route than taking others she was toying with.

One day, she was talking with a professor about her recent standardized test scores and he assured her that she did not have what it would take to become a nurse. It must have been devastating to hear such a negative message while pursuing her career. My mom… Well, let's just say she didn't care what that professor had to say because she knew her truth.

It's important to speak our truths into existence. It helps us overcome anything negative that others may speak about us. We are in control of our identities and what we believe about ourselves. We just need to learn how to filter the negative voices that may come our way.

She knew in her heart that nursing was what she was called to do. My mother became a nurse, then a manager, then the head of a children's hospital, and eventually the CEO of seven hospitals under one umbrella. She helped change the idea of what healthcare should look like, never listening to that professor who only spoke negatives into her life. She chose to prove him wrong and conquer the healthcare field.

My mother went back to that professor eventually, and told him he should never crush another person's goals and essentially tell them they don't have what it takes. She sure proved him wrong. I admire my mother in so many ways, not because she was successful in her career but because she had the values and standards that are important in life.

Being true to yourself is showing others your authenticity. It's realizing your greatest, deepest needs and allowing yourself to embrace them.

She is a shining example of owning your truth, loving God, loving others where they are, and lifting people up when they need it the most. It's funny because I hear a lot of people say they will never turn out like their mother or father, but the truth is, if I am even half the woman my mother is, I would be so thankful.

The next time an obstacle stands in your way, such as a person simply telling you that you can't achieve something, look them dead in the eye and say, "Thanks for your opinion. However, it wasn't asked for." Okay, you don't necessarily need to say it that way, but you get the point. No one should tell you that you can't accomplish something because you are not qualified.

A simple exercise I commonly use with clients to help them challenge their negative self-beliefs is what I like to refer to as "Speak into the Mirror." I give someone a blank piece of paper and lots of crayons because colors make everything better and brighter. On this piece of paper, I ask that they write positive truth statements about themselves, even if they don't fully believe these truths yet. On mine, I would write, "I am good enough. I am an awesome mother. I am beautiful. I am strong. I am worthy." These are just a few examples, but it gives you the idea. When I run, which is something I haven't done in a long time, I scream these words out loud to motivate myself to run just a little bit further. People I have passed must have thought I was absolutely crazy, but I don't care. I'm not trying to sound cocky at all here, so follow me.

The real work begins when you are consistent in speaking truths into your life. I'll simply ask clients to take their paper full of positive messages about themselves and tape it to their mirror. Every single day they look into the mirror and recite the statements out loud. I love this exercise because it instills positive statements into your existence. You are creating your identity with beautiful self-beliefs. The more you say the statements out loud, the more you will come to believe them. The more you come to believe them, the more confidence you will have in yourself.

It doesn't matter what other people's opinions are of you, its none of your business. What matters most is your opinion of yourself. Remember that misery loves company. I think this is one of the reasons I have had a hard time maintaining close friendships.

I tend to have a bubbly and outgoing personality, and, believe it or not, there are quite a few people out there who don't share in this delight. Don't subject yourself to falling down the trap of negative beliefs and negative self-talk. You are so much more than that. You are amazing! You are wonderful! You are you!

Take the time to surround yourself with the positives in your life. Of course we will have ups and downs. Of course we will have moments when we need to sit with our hard feelings. But that's just it: sit with your emotions, whether they are good or bad. Allow yourself to absorb your surroundings. Look for the different perspectives in every situation to allow yourself to be surrounded by people who will encourage you and lift you up.

It is important to be true to yourself and also to be true to others. If your words or silence are going to harm another person or hurt their feelings, then they will most likely not accept hearing the truth. There needs to be a healthy balance to also help preserve relationships. This is especially true in marriage. I have heard the saying, "Never let the sun set on your anger." I don't know about you but I think this is very good advice. Giving the silent treatment to your significant other can be detrimental. It builds resentment and allows all of the little things that bother you to build up inside until you finally explode. This, my friends, is not being fair to each other. It's not being truthful to each other, and it's definitely not being a positive influence on each other.

What matters most is your opinion of yourself.

Live within your personal values, do not intend to harm others, and accept your life truths so that you are not compromising yourself or anyone else. Your decision to be a trustworthy soul will reflect loudly in the way you live your life and treat others.

Four Reasons it's better to tell the truth:

It gives others empowerment: When we tell someone the truth about themselves or a situation they are in, it empowers the other person to create a change in themselves or their lives if needed.

It preserves your integrity: Remaining true to who you are and your values will give you a sense of pride in knowing you have not compromised yourself.

It earns you respect: When other people can count on you to tell the truth, they will develop respect for who you are as a person. Telling the truth will let other people know you truly care for them.

It shows love for other people: People innately try to control and manipulate others and their surroundings. When you tell the truth, you are showing people your authentic love for them.

CHAPTER TWELVE

Dance It Out Girl

Imagine this: The house looks like a tornado just ripped through each and every single room. It's only seven in the morning, and the baby is lifting her arms up to be held. The coffee was brewing, but I forgot about it and now it's cold. I hate the taste of reheated coffee. My son is complaining that he can't find anything good to eat for breakfast. My daughter is already asking me what we are having for dinner and pleading her case for chicken nuggets and mac 'n' cheese. The toddler, well, she is two, so she is throwing a fit about something I did or didn't do.

The laundry has piled so high that it now looks like a volcano about to explode more than it already has. The bills are in a stack, and I hope they aren't overdue yet. However, something tells me they are close. The dishes are at least soaking in the sink. That has to count for something, right?

I could pull from a million different coping skills here. I could lock myself in my bedroom, get lost in a book, become absorbed in social media, or even grab a glass of wine (I know it's the morning. Don't judge. Remember Chapter One on judgment?) Half the time, I live on coffee in the morning to get going and wine at night to settle down. Anyway, during the day, I choose to turn to something a little more upbeat: some country music (or... "Baby Shark"). I grab my kids by the hand and dance it out! I get moving and grooving, and I look like a fool, but you know what, it makes me feel a whole lot better. In that silly moment, I can let go and let loose all of my worries, well, until my kids look at me funny because I am trying to teach them the "Cha Cha Slide."

We all have ways we choose to cope with daily life. We are all, in a sense, addicted to something that makes us feel better. The question is, Are you addicted to healthy methods of coping or unhealthy ones? It may seem like a funny question, but some coping methods that may seem healthy at first can quickly get out of control.

Coping skills are resources we use to help us deal with a stressor. Everyone has coping skills they turn to on a daily basis. A lot of our skills were taught to us when we were young children. It's a generational pattern that does have the ability to be broken if needed. When we become parents, we are equipped with an invisible tool bag passed to us by each of our parents. I have one and my husband has one too. You have one and your significant other has one. No one tool bag is the same, but there are tools we pull from that we have seen our parents use during their times of stress.

I think this may be part of the reason I am so horrible with grief. I know everyone has a difficult time with grief because it's never easy when you lose someone you love. I personally don't think I had the tools to know how to grieve.

I lost my grandmother on my mother's side when I was just five years old. She had been living with us because she was battling cancer. I used to love coming home from school and putting on dance shows for her by standing on the ledge of our fireplace and dancing my heart out. Maybe this is why I like to "dance it out" now when I feel stressed. One day, I came home from spending the night at my other grandmother's house and found that my grandma who was sick had passed. When I saw my mother, she was hysterical and almost couldn't breathe.

I remember feeling so scared, so I ran to the window and said, "Mommy, she forgot to bring her car with her to heaven."

I had no idea how to respond. I was only five, but I knew I felt sad and scared. I didn't want to make things worse for my mother by interfering with her grief. I refrained from asking questions and was not allowed to attend my grandmother's funeral. My mother became depressed and withdrawn during that time. I don't blame her but it was so hard for me as well. A year later, I lost my grandfather, and I remember feeling so numb. I am so fortunate that, to date, I have only lost two people very close to me, and I was at a very young age when they passed. However, the thought of losing someone close to me now terrifies me. I don't know how to grieve. I know there isn't one correct way to grieve, but I pull from the toolbox I watched my mom pull from when she lost her mother. I know I will need to work through this more, and I have been. It's a slow process to retrain your brain.

My husband and I were once on a bike ride with our little girls to get some food when we received a call telling us one of our very close friends had passed after suffering from a heart attack. We were standing outside at a sushi restaurant, and I fell to the floor, sobbing. It was confirmed later by another person and then another that our friend was gone. It was a complete shock and came out of nowhere. He was young and healthy. We had just spoken with him two days prior.

When we got home, after what seemed like the longest bike ride ever, neither my husband nor I could eat, let alone talk. I placed the food bag on the counter, and then chopsticks fell out. As I picked them up, I noticed they were each taken out of the package, broken apart, and connected back together into what resembled crosses. I don't know if it was the considerate thoughts of the people at the restaurant or the idea that this could have been a sign that our friend was safe in heaven, but I felt comforted. This was something I had never felt before when in a state of grief.

Some people will choose to turn to alcohol or drugs or food or something else to numb the pain. It's a Band-Aid that gets ripped off each time the effects subside. A common coping method I see in my practice is self-harm. This is a type of coping method I believe is so important to address, especially because I work with a lot of people who self-injure. It's important to note that the type of self-injury I am talking about is the non-suicidal type.

When people choose to harm themselves, it is often impulsive. Self-harm can be anything from cutting, scratching, burning, or even bruising oneself. It's hard to believe that anyone would want to intentionally hurt themselves, but the type of harm I am talking about releases endorphins and increases serotonin levels so that relief is felt instead of pain. I know this sounds weird and is almost difficult to imagine, but that is how it works. Cutting oneself offers the same release as working out does.

A method commonly used to help individuals pinpoint the trigger for self-injury or any other addictive behavior used for coping is the string technique. A person is given a piece of string and asked to tie a knot in the string to symbolize when they were born, another knot to symbolize how old they are now, and one more knot to symbolize the first time of engaging in self-injury or the addictive behavior. The trigger is most likely not around the time when the addictive behavior started but the year before, so a fourth knot is made to indicate that. This can be a good indicator and starting point for trying to figure out the source of the behaviors.

I am often asked by these clients' loved ones how they can help others cope with self-injury or any other mental illness. I believe this is an important question because while coping mechanisms are important for the individual to learn themselves, others can also assist with healthy coping techniques. Some of the most important ways you can help are to stay calm, offer non-judgmental remarks, focus on the underlying feelings and issues rather than the behaviors themselves, be empathetic, not threaten hospitalization, try not to reprimand, avoid displaying shock or showing pity, and help plan for safety.

There are a lot of unhealthy and destructive coping skills we can and will choose to use. There are also a lot of healthier ways we can use, but even they can become out of hand if done excessively. A good example of this is when people choose to throw themselves into their work. Working, in general, is not a bad thing to invest in, but when it comes to a point where you might be considered a workaholic and it interferes with other aspects of your life, it becomes an unhealthy way of coping. I know so many people who tell me that they are amazing at their jobs, and this is wonderful, but then they tell me they work every chance they get because they feel it is the only aspect of their life that they excel at.

Let's give another practical example: working out. Exercise is an amazing release for stress. It releases those good-feeling hormones that we all need. There needs to be a balance, though. A balance between the amount of exercise quantity and quality. There are too many instances of excessive exercise turning into eating disorders in individuals who are already predisposed. This just creates another issue to have to work through.

One coping method I love to use, however, is the "peaks, pits, praises and prayers" journal. Journaling is an awesome way to express your feelings and reprocess your emotions. I tend to find it a little tedious to write a full-on journal, so I try to condense it a little. I write in a journal I have created and list my favorite part of the day, my worst part of the day, the things I was most thankful for, and the prayers I have for myself and other people. I also take it a step further, and each night before bed, we ask our kids what their favorite part of the day was and what their least favorite part of the day was. Using this with kids is a great way to gain insight into their days. A lot of parents will only ask their kids if their day was good. This is a closed-ended question that allows kids to answer in a yes or no fashion. By asking an open-ended question, you will most likely be able to gain more information into how their day was.

It's imperative, when you find yourself in the heat of the moment, to remind yourself to stay calm. Without calmness, your brain can't enter into the rational side of thinking long enough to come up with a good coping method. Other great skills I hope you will consider choosing from are: writing, doing crossword puzzles, getting out into nature, talking with a friend, letting yourself cry, playing with a pet, shopping, making images out of the clouds, listening to music, praying, meditating, and one of my favorites, choosing a childhood activity, such as swinging on a swing or coloring. Of course, the list can go on and on but if any of these resonate with you, then I would like to encourage you to make a spinning wheel with these different examples so that when you need it the most, you can just spin the wheel and go.

Forget your troubles and dance[1]

Bob Marley

Moving Forward

If there is one thing my dad tried to instill in me and my sister time and time again, it was to have persistence and to never give up. In my childhood home, there used to be a canvas with a lot of short phrases that offered encouragement. I couldn't tell you any other words on there except for one short but powerful phrase. Persistence, persistence, persistence.

Persistence is considered a personality trait that people exhibit when they push through a hard time despite feeling fatigued or frustrated. Good Lord, I know as a mother I feel like I need to push through almost each and every day! Without the mindset of never giving up, we might not have accomplished the very thing that helped make us who we are as individuals.

I am often amazed at the amount of persistence kids have. Let me paint you a picture. We have just sat down as a family for dinner and in front of my kids is a healthy dish of protein, vegetables, and rice. I don't know how you do it in your home, but we have really tried to have everyone eat the same meal so that we are not making multiple meals—one meal for my husband and I and then one for each kid, which usually ended up being mostly processed foods. Dinner always started off with my husband and I telling the kids they need to eat what is on their plates. In return, we were given multiple rounds of our kids trying to negotiate. They'd ask us, "Can I just eat this and not that?" or "Can I just eat half of this?" After what seemed like hours of negotiating (persistence on our kids' part), we got so tired and, sometimes, gave in.

I feel like we can learn a lot from these tiny humans. Granted, they do not know the meaning of struggles and hard times yet, but their foundation in moving forward is strong. This will stay with them throughout their lives. It is inevitable that we will fall and feel like we have failed. It is inevitable that we will, at some point, be tempted to just quit. However, I encourage you to use each fall as a learning experience and not an excuse to give up.

We teach our kids this all the time. A good example is teaching children how to ride a bike without training wheels. What would we be teaching our kids if we let them give up after they fell off of their bike and decided to quit? Get them back on that bike and have them try again and again until they soar down that road.

I know of some friends who refuse to push forward out of fear of either failure or success. That sounds a little weird, so let me explain. Each of us has a different idea of what success looks like in our lives. Some of us want to run a multimillion dollar company. Some of us long to be able to stay home with our children while they are young and not have to worry about the bills. Either way, success is a personal goal. It can be scary to take the next step and enter the unknown. The idea of pushing forward toward achievement can bring out the perfectionist in people. If their work isn't validated, it will inevitably hold them back. News flash, we are not perfect. Our work will not be perfect and anyone who feels the need to judge others needs to take a hard look at themselves.

Persistence can be so hard when we are deep into self-doubt or feeling depressed. These feelings steal our motivation and desire to want to try any further. I have often had to explain this to parents when their teenagers enter into my office and are showing signs of depression. The scene usually plays out with the parents explaining that they are concerned for their child because they have been sad and isolative, and their thoughts are in a dark place. They then proceed on about how their grades have slipped and that is one thing that is "unacceptable." I don't know about you, but I have had seasons of feeling depressed and didn't want to do anything, much less get out of bed. I could get parents to understand a little better when comparing this to depression in adults and not wanting to go to work. Now, an adult will most likely push through, but maybe they are short with their co-workers and their work quality decreases, similar to how a child's grades slip. Teenagers who are depressed need help learning how to push forward but they also need to be validated in their emotions.

I have to work on this concept myself. I remember when I was having a tough day and my bed looked extra comfy in the mid-morning. I had to decide if I wanted to give in, crawl back into bed, and let my girls crawl all over me while I tried to just close my eyes or if I had enough strength in me to move forward with the day. I decided, if I made my bed, then I would be less tempted to wallow. I then got dressed and started my day. Sometimes doing the harder thing feels so much better at the end of the day.

Admiral William McRaven once said that if you make your bed every morning and have a crappy day, at least you will come home to a bed that is made.[1] You have accomplished the first task of the day, and you are more likely to accomplish more tasks throughout the day.

Another area where the world seems to be moving in a fast forward motion is in the social media realm. So many advances are being made through online interactions and it can be difficult to keep up with them. Teenagers are especially engaged in the social media life and can be persistent in obtaining the newest applications so that they are well connected with their peers.

Back in the good old days, when I was younger, life seemed much simpler. It seemed like there was a little less pressure from the outside world. I had the internet, but it was more like the dial-up speed, and instead of social media, we engaged in chat rooms. I have to laugh at it now because when I was a kid, we all thought there couldn't be anything better. Now we have Facebook, Instagram, Snapchat, etc. Social media has made a world of a difference when it comes to connecting with friends and family who are not local. It allows for easy ways to share pictures and stories. It is even good for growing your business. Unfortunately, it also has given access to predators and cyberbullies, which has led children to take their own lives or the lives of others. I feel it's important to look at a couple of these applications and sites so parents are a little more aware of the ever-changing social media culture that has our society on fast forward.

Moving Forward in the Social Media World

Some of the most commonly used applications are Facebook, Twitter, Snapchat, and Tumblr. Teens are starting to steer away from Facebook, Twitter, and Tumblr due to the adult population taking them over more and more every day. So I have decided not to include these common applications because most people know of them and the risks associated with them. I want to inform you of the newer applications kids and teens are starting to download.

Tinder: This is a dating application commonly referred to as a "hook up" app. It allows users to view pictures, mostly from Facebook and Instagram. Users will then either swipe left to indicate a dislike or swipe right to indicate a like. When both parties swipe right, they are "matched." There have been multiple reports of violence and sexual assault from individuals who have met others on Tinder. There is also no way of knowing if the person you are talking to has made a fake profile and is a predator waiting for the right opportune moment to attack.

Whisper: Whisper is a social networking site where users are given a random username so that their identity remains anonymous. This site is famous for people posting confessions using text and photos. The application shares your location within a one-mile radius to other users. Because of the shared location, it makes it easier for online predators to contact users. This application can also be used to share personal information, allow for cyberbullying, and use intimidation for revenge.

Jailbreaking apps: These are scary! They are intended for users to be able to hide applications within their phone so that they are not accessible on the home screen of the phone. This can also be done without jailbreaking, but the process involves having to redo it every time your phone is restarted. Because this process is more in-depth, I'll let you look it up for more details.

I know that possibly months from now, the applications I have listed will be out of date, and there will probably be even more dangerous ones. That is hard to imagine, but technology is constantly evolving and getting scarier by the day. It's important to educate ourselves and to also educate our children on these dangers and how to avoid them. Not only are we constantly moving forward and growing personally, but our world is moving at a fast forward pace with or without us.

It's so easy to become a victim of bullying or even a Tinder date gone wrong, but be strong in who you are. There are going to be many sharks in this world whose mission is to attack you, put you down and take things from you. Kill them with kindness. Remember that we don't know what other people are going through in their life, but we can choose how we respond to them. Don't get stuck where you currently are in life. Accept the challenge and keep going. Have persistence.

CHAPTER FOURTEEN

It's Never Too Late

Life is short. One day we will wake up and realize there are things we still want to do but may feel our time is limited. I want you to know that as long as you are alive it is never too late to accomplish new things.

It's never too late to take the high road. Imagine getting into a fight or disagreement with someone, and the next thing you know, you are seeing little jabs on their Facebook page that are clearly directed at you but don't actually tag your name. I know it takes a lot to not make any comments back, but take the higher road of silence. It is a killer.

It's never too late to go back to school. I admire teen mothers who chose to keep their babies but didn't give up their goals of completing high school or going to college to better themselves. It's so hard to be a mother, let alone a single teen mom. Bravo, mamas! Your children will one day recognize your amazing sacrifice and devotion to your family. You are awesome!

It's also never too late to leave toxic relationships. I love the quote by author Jennifer Green, who said, "Sometimes you need to give up on people, not because you don't care but because they don't care."[1] I have had my fair share of toxic friendships, and I have tried to salvage them many times. The best thing I ever did for my health and sanity was to realize it was time to burn those bridges and go separate ways. I don't—we don't—need that negativity or criticism. We don't need people who waste our time, people who walk all over us, people who disappoint us time and time again, friends who are jealous of us and our lives, people who are self-centered, and people who just don't give a damn. Here is your permission. Let those people go. You will be happier for it.

It's never too late to apologize. It takes a bigger person to apologize than to just walk away. Apologizing doesn't mean you are always saying sorry for something that you did wrong. Sometimes a simple "I'm sorry" opens the door to better communication. Of course, there are times when we can say something or do something that upsets another person. The key is to never let the sun set on your anger. Even if you feel you are not in the wrong, you can let your guard down enough to allow the other person to feel safe enough to talk openly with you.

It's never too late to reconnect with someone. People come in and out of our lives for a reason, sometimes for a season and sometimes for a lifetime. Each interaction we have teaches us something about ourselves or our lives. If someone has been out of your life for a while but you find yourself needing and/or wanting their wisdom, then reconnect. People crave friendship and community. Who knows, you may have just developed a beautiful, deep friendship.

It's never too late to make a change. Don't like your career path? Go back to school, learn a trade, apply for a new job. Want to get healthier? Learn how to run, choose healthier eating options, exercise, take your vitamins, get some sunshine, and drink half your body weight in ounces of water a day. Hate the place you live in? You only get one life. Choose to be happy and live where you will love each and every day. You can change almost anything you want. Don't let anything stand in your way. You've got this.

It's never too late to walk away from things that make you unhappy. I have come to realize that I used to spend so much time and energy with everything that came my way. I wasn't feeling joyful. My mood was affected and I could feel the anxiety build. To help combat this, I made a point to spend more quality time with my family and friends and less time on social media. I gave up commitments that interfered with my time or my family time. Learn to recognize what it is that you do that is making you unhappy and choose to walk away.

It's never too late to do the right thing. Listen, this one is hard. Not everyone will agree on what the "right thing" is. The important part for you to remember is to stay true to yourself and your beliefs. Always ask yourself about your motives and intentions. In every situation, do what you feel and believe is the right choice. You won't regret it.

It's never too late to learn to love yourself. I don't know about you, but I'm pretty sick and tired of society dictating what I need to do and look like for other people to like me. I am not a size two and I'm still alive and happy. I have learned as long as you are taking care of yourself, then you are loving yourself. You are amazing! You are beautiful! You are you!

It's never too late to let go of resentment. It takes a bigger person to let go of those resentful feelings toward someone else. Resentment makes you bitter. It makes you harbor anger. Letting go of resentment makes room for more freedom. It's not allowing others to keep a hold on you. It's taking back control of your life.

It's never too late to be bold. Forget the traditional mainstream standards set by society. You don't have to follow them if you don't want to. I love the character Penelope Cruz from the show Criminal Minds. While everyone else is dressed in neutral colors, she comes out in her wild and bold attire of bright colors, holding a fluffy pen.

By all means, you don't have to go that bold if it's not your style, but don't be afraid to be bold and stand out from the crowd. God tells us to live in this world but not be of this world.

It's never too late to take a nap. Yep, you read that one right. Slow down, girl. Take time to rest and rejuvenate. Your body will tell you exactly what it needs in order to function. Listen to your body and calm your soul. Grab your little ones and go take a nap. You have permission.

It's never too late to make peace with yourself, others, and your past. You have spent years developing who you are as a person. Each experience you have gone through has shaped you. Each success you have achieved, has created the you that you see. Don't forget to give yourself and others the grace you each deserve. Life is too short to hold onto negative experiences from your past. It is too short to stay around people who have done you wrong. Let go and choose to be happy.

It's never too late to find a therapist. Just because you can benefit from talking to a third party about life does not qualify you as being mentally unstable. It makes you smart. It makes you healthy. It will help give you life skills to be a better adult. Heck, even therapists have their own therapist. I love mine!

It is never too late to say "I love you." Swallow your pride. Let go of that stubbornness. Those three little words are meant to be said and heard by all. It makes you and others feel loved, appreciated, important, and connected. Don't ever let your anger get the best of you and withhold these words from your loved ones and friends. You will never regret telling someone you love them.

It's never too late to learn from your mistakes. Remember when I said that you can learn from your failures instead of giving up? Sometimes, it feels like I take one step ahead and then two steps back but in the end it was a good learning experience.

I have found myself saying, multiple times a week, "My darling daughter, you have now lost your tablet, access to the playroom, and your bike for the next several days. I don't appreciate you lying to me every night about brushing your teeth. And no, brushing without toothpaste does not mean you actually did brush your teeth."

I finally learned that negative reinforcement does not work with kids. I should have known this because, as a therapist, I preach this to parents. It seems like parenting is so much harder when it's your own children.

We finally turned toward a positive reward system that involves rocks. Each kid received their own mason jar, and as they were complemented by an adult or their sibling for doing something nice or helping out, they got one rock put into their jar. If they had a total of ten rocks by the end of the week, they got to go to the awesome treasure chest filled with dollar store goodies. Of course, they could lose rocks throughout the week as well. They lost a rock if their attitudes were not respectful, they didn't listen, they were mean to their sibling(s), and other things. This method may work for a time, but as children get older or get bored of it, you will have to get creative and change things up.

In the end, remember it is never too late to make a change.

Ways to make changes in your life:

Make a decision and stick to it: It is easy to go back and forth on decisions you have made but try not to. You will feel more confident in yourself if you make a decision and follow through with it.

Surround yourself with positive people: All of the it's never too late statements that you have read above would not be possible to do if you don't have people in your life who will lift you up and encourage you. Remove negativity and allow yourself the permission to do the things in your life that bring you joy.

Learn something new: It is important to challenge yourself every day. Change your mindset about learning by making it fun. You can google a fun fact, do a puzzle, talk to a new person. Keep your brain active and you will feel rejuvenated.

Be authentic: Be who you are and don't change yourself for other people. When you are your true self other people will see you are genuine and will be more likely to be accepting of you.

Bring out your inner-child: You may be an adult but make sure you make the time to have fun again, like when you were a kid. You can help to reduce stress in your life when you learn to let go a little. You can play hide and seek, color, swing on a swing, or just get outside and play.

We always may be what we might have been.[2]

Adelaide Anne Procter

CHAPTER FIFTEEN

Breaking Free

Almost my entire family is in healthcare. My mother started as a nurse. My sister is a nurse manager. My aunt started out as a nurse, and my sister in law is an ultrasound technician. Seemed like big shoes to fill. Growing up, healthcare surrounded me. We were constantly at the local pediatric hospital, where my mother worked at the time as president of the hospital. We would hang out there and play in the atrium where there was a huge castle and a statue of the genie from Aladdin! They eventually took it down because kids of the younger generation don't know who the genie is. Crazy! This sure makes me feel old.

It wasn't expected of me and my sister to go into the medical aspect of the healthcare field, and in fact, my parents were very supportive in helping us develop and find our own way. It was, however, not frowned upon to follow in the footsteps of the family who were in the medical healthcare field. I thought about it when I was younger, but even the thought of seeing someone else's blood made me nauseous. And don't even mention veins to me. They are so gross. Needless to say, the physical side of the healthcare field was not my calling. This was made very clear by my teenage years, when I struggled with a lot of mental health issues, such as anxiety and depression. It was working through this time of struggles that I realized I was meant to be a mental health counselor and not a medical nurse.

In a sense, by making my own decision, I felt like I was breaking free from pressure that I had placed on myself. I allowed myself to follow my heart and passion. If you have ever felt stuck, done something in your life only because you felt it was expected of you, or have gone down a path only to please other people, then let me be the loud voice in your life that tells you to finally break free and be who you were meant to be.

I love the song "Where You Are" in the movie Moana. Moana's father is the chief of the village, and Moana is next in line to lead her people. The problem is that Moana does not feel called to stay on the island. She is drawn to the water, just like her grandmother was. Moana's father tells her that their people will one day need a chief and that is who she is meant to be. He tells her that the island provides all she needs, that there is no need to look elsewhere. Later, we see Moana next to her grandmother dancing near the water's edge. Her grandmother shares with her that she loves the water because it misbehaves. She encourages her to respect her parents but to also not lose sight of who she is.

This is a great reminder that when we are young, our care-givers are laying the foundation for us. They help guide us and, hopefully, bring us up to know our full potential. While I am sure we are all grateful for them, we are the only ones who can truly know what and who we were meant to be. And once we are adults, we will continue to break free and make choices for ourselves and our lives.

Don't live out someone else's ideas for your life. Let's face it, life can become monotonous. It can get tiring doing the same thing day in and day out. It can be rewarding and draining all at the same time. Don't get me wrong, I love routines. Routines help me make it through the day with greater ease. But it's also important to remember to live a little by being spontaneous and allowing others to leave their positive mark on your life.

Surround yourself with positive, uplifting people. Engage yourself with strong women who will offer different perspectives about life. If you stay within the bubble of what is comfortable, you are only limiting yourself. You are fogging your judgment by only allowing yourself to stay within the confines of what you already know and are aware of.

Surround yourself with people who have a good heart. My dad taught me this from a young age. He always told us that it didn't matter who we chose to be our significant other as long as they treated us well and had a good heart.

I don't think people were born innately good. I believe, because of the fall of man, we were all born into sin. It is a daily choice to be happy and genuine. Having said that, it's very difficult to find genuine people to surround yourself with, people who truly have a heart of gold. It's hard to find friends who can put themselves aside, truly listen, and be there for you. Follow your instinct with friends. You will feel who is genuine and who is being fake. Don't waste your time with anyone who is fake with you. Don't make someone your priority while allowing yourself to be their option. You deserve better than that.

Don't be so consumed with what everyone else around you is doing either; it shouldn't matter to you. You are your own person with your own set of skills. You are unique, and there is no one the same as you. Chances are, when you were a kid, you probably begged your parents to extend your curfew by half an hour because everyone else's curfew was later than yours. Chances are also good that you may have asked for a cell phone when you were twelve years old because everyone else had one. Heck, at only eight years old, my son was already begging me for a phone. When I asked him who he would call, he said, "I don't know, but everyone else my age has one." Um, no, sir. I am sure there are plenty of eight-year-olds running around without a cell phone.

When these kinds of situations pop up, many children hear, "Well, if your friends jumped off a bridge, would you?" Of course the answer is no—unless the child was stubborn and answered yes. The point is, you don't have to be just like everyone else around you. You don't have to try to "fit in." In fact, I think some of the most fascinating people are the ones who stand bold in who they are. Especially as adults, we don't have to worry as much about bullying and, by golly, we should know by now how to stand up for ourselves should we ever need to.

Going against the grain will most definitely cause resistance with other people. Most people shy away from things that make them feel uncomfortable or things that they cannot themselves understand. Eventually, when people see you living your life to the fullest and how happy it makes you, they will long for that type of life and happiness as well. You will then have been a wonderful example to the majority of people in this society.

I don't want you to think I am telling you to go out of your way to be different than everyone else, but if it's truly what you want to do, then by all means, you go, girl. Get tattoo sleeves, wear an all-black or a neon outfit, put on bold makeup. You don't have to buy the most up-to-date "stylish" outfit or five-inch heels (but go for it if that's truly what you want). Don't try to be different or try to fit in just for the sake of it. Just be you. Do what makes you happy. Be who makes you happy.

The second you start to feel content in life, you have stopped growing and learning. Look for new ways each day to challenge yourself so you can grow personally. Imagine, as a parent, realizing it was time to put your little one in a "big kid" bed. This is a big step for parents as well as the child. It can also be a brutal time for parents. The crib is a safe place. It's a place where you know you can put your little one to rest and be assured the next morning that they will be right where you put them—unless, of course, they have learned how to climb out. The thing is, it's inevitable that the time will come when your baby has grown up to the point of wanting and needing more freedom. They will break free from the baby crib and enter into a whole new world where chaos ensues but learning and growing expands.

This can be said with many milestones in life while growing up. It's important to not forget that learning and growing can still happen even after you become an established adult. Your brain doesn't fully stop growing until your about twenty-five years old. Think about that for a second. That means every decision you have made up to the point of full brain maturity was made with limitations. This is part of the reason why teenagers can be so moody. The part of the brain that develops first is the amygdala, which deals with emotions, impulsiveness, and aggression. They haven't yet fully developed the prefrontal cortex, which helps with planning and decision making. The cool thing, though, is that even after we are twenty-five, we have the ability to change our brains by learning and experiencing new things. We just have to have the desire to keep pushing ourselves to become better than we were the day before.

Let's let go of what society thinks is "normal." Let's stop trying to fit into a mold of how others think we should live our lives. What works well for me may not work well for you, and that is okay. To each their own.

Freedom is the power to choose your own chains.

Jean Jacques Rousseau

CHAPTER SIXTEEN

Better Than Yesterday

I have full-on yelled at my kids before. I'm not talking about raising my voice. I'm talking about speaking so incredibly loud that you could hardly understand what I was saying. And after I was done, my throat hurt. I wouldn't even be surprised if my neighbors could hear me. I hate this version of myself. Sometimes, my limits are just pushed to that point. Kids really know how to test boundaries and to the fullest extent. When I have those moments, or even those days, I try to remember to extend myself a little grace and think to myself that there is always tomorrow, God willing.

I personally have things I need to do each day in order to feel good about myself, physically and emotionally. I know that if I don't eat a healthy breakfast, drink my coffee, take my vitamins, and get some exercise each and every day, then my day feels crappy. I feel crappy. Of course, I have those days when I just need to sit and do diddly squat, but I don't get those days very often. My mother-in-law liked to joke with me,

We won't be perfect all day, every day. We will stumble and have moments of weakness. That's what our tomorrows are for.

and on the days I was home with my kids, she would call me up and say, "Watcha doing? Sitting around eating bonbons?" She knew full well that with two toddlers running around, I was anything but sitting down. And the day just kept getting crazier after the other two came home from school. There came the meltdowns and the homework (oh, the homework). There was fixing dinner, unloading backpacks and lunchboxes, preparing lunches for the next day, and doing bedtime routines. While I loved all of this, it got overwhelming at times.

We won't be perfect all day, every day. We will stumble and have moments of weakness. That's what our tomorrows are for. We are not promised our tomorrows but, God willing, we will be here to have another day on this earth and another day to make a difference on this earth and in the lives of others. One of my major prayers is that God will allow me to stay on this earth to raise my little ones. It breaks my heart hearing about those families whose adult loved ones were taken too early from this world and, even worse, children who have passed well before their time.

Instead of focusing on the struggles or down pits of the day, we should allow ourselves to shake it off and give it another go. It's easy to throw in the towel. What's difficult is taking that towel, cleaning it, and using it again for something even better. I once heard that "worry ends where faith begins." We have a sign with these words hanging over our entryway, and every time I go through the doorway, I feel a sense of hope and peace. I think of it as starting over each time I pass under it.

I recently completed a trauma training course called Reconsolidation of Traumatic Memories or RTM. I am trained in other trauma therapies as well, and, going into this training, I was a bit skeptical. I actually did not want to attend this training but was convinced to attend by a friend of mine, and I am really glad I did. This protocol is used on a lot of military veterans who have come home from war and are experiencing Post-Traumatic Stress Disorder (PTSD). I have personally seen big guys who have served in our military not be able to talk about the traumatic experiences they had while away at war. I have seen these men become emotionally charged and even seen some start to cry. After just the first session using the RTM protocol, I saw these men transform into men who could tell their stories flawlessly and in great detail with no negative emotions attached. If you think about it, these veterans are people who didn't know if they had any tomorrows, not necessarily because of death looming over them but because the amount of trauma they experienced caused severe PTSD, and daily life became debilitating.

Of course, I had to experience this "treatment" for myself too. Witnessing the transformation just wasn't enough for my brain. I had just been through a traumatic experience myself, so why not try it out, right? I had the privilege of participating in the live demonstration for the RTM protocol during our training session. I decided it was as good a time as any to focus on the traumatic birth experience of my youngest daughter. I sat in front of a room of trainees and let myself experience the RTM treatment. It took me forty-five minutes to complete the first session. By the end of that time, I was able to tell about my labor experience in great detail without feeling any negative emotions attached to my story. I was absolutely amazed. This protocol changed my view of my birth experience. I have since then started using this protocol in my practice and even on friends I know who can benefit from the therapy.

I love that we have things in this world that can give us hope for our future. I would like to encourage you to find what helps you. For me, clearing some past hurts and taking care of myself has allowed me to move forward in a more positive way. If you are interested, you, too, can hear my story on episode twenty-five of the podcast Life After PTSD and see if this might be a therapy that might benefit you.

Despite having things that can help us get through hard times, we also have the ability inside ourselves to make positive changes. Our brains are amazing. They have the ability to, in a sense, trick ourselves into believing things we would otherwise not necessarily believe in. My husband personally likes to think of the field I am in as being a bit manipulative. While I can see his point, I don't believe psychology was meant to manipulate other people. Instead, I believe people have it within themselves to make the changes needed to allow themselves to be the best person they can be.

A lot of people become compliant in their daily lives and don't realize that change can actually be a good thing. It's important to recognize the very traits about yourself that you want to change to make a better difference in your life. For me, having patience with myself allows me to take a step back and determine what I feel is important for me to take away from the day. I believe we can learn from our everyday experiences and change the parts we believe to be unfavorable. Had I not gone out of my comfort zone and attended the RTM training, I would still be struggling with depression, panic attacks, and much more.

I believe in personal motivation and change so much that in my practice, I don't let my clients leave the office without setting some personal goals to work toward for the week. Having something tangible allows for motivation and accountability. I love seeing my clients a week later, after they accomplished what they set out to do. The intrinsic reward they get instills the idea that they have the control to change their lives for the better.

Ask yourself what you liked about yourself today. Maybe it was simply showing up for your family. Maybe it was setting aside time to be productive. Whatever it is you accomplished, take joy and be proud of yourself. Be proud that you showed up. Tomorrow, add to your success by setting out to accomplish another goal. Your goals don't have to be big by any means. Just make sure you live each day with passion, joy, thankfulness, and motivation. When you show up and are present, being the best person you know how to be, your tomorrows will be filled with a life you can be proud of. Go get it, girl. The world is yours and no one can stop you.

If today you are a little better than you were yesterday, then that is enough.[1]

David A. Bednar

CHAPTER SEVENTEEN

Confidence

As women, I feel like confidence and self-esteem can be really hard to accomplish. They are also some of the most important traits women can adopt, especially because society ingrains in us that we need to be a certain way in order to be accepted. I wish women would come together and support each other instead of feeling like they need to compete with each other. I think that is part of the reason I tended to get along much better with males when I was younger. I wasn't a tomboy as a teenager but I always felt more accepted around guys. I didn't feel like I had to be involved in drama and defend myself to the popular girls.

I hated high school. I mean I HATED high school. I went to an awesome private school, but I never quite felt like I fit in well. Actually, I got along better with the people in the grade above me because they were more down to earth than the people in my grade. Of course, when the grade above me graduated, I was left feeling like an outcast again. I can't even recall anyone being

This is your world. You can either choose to mold it the way you want, or someone else will do it for you.

mean to me. I just didn't fit in with my class' standards. Unfortunately, at the time, I didn't have the awareness to not care and just be myself.

Now, as an adult, we still have to deal with these kinds of people, but, hopefully, we have gotten to the point in our lives where we can just brush it off and move on. People who are mean to you are only jealous, and the reality is, they fear that they will never be able to get to where you are now. Don't let anyone steal your confidence in yourself or your abilities. This is your world. You can either choose to mold it the way you want, or someone else will do it for you.

I wonder if, at some point in our lives, we started out confident, but due to our environment, we were conditioned to question it. I believe negative life events and having a sense of lack of control contributes largely to this. I also believe it can be reversed. We were put on this earth for a reason, and every day we are given is a blessing. We need to utilize our gifts for the good of others. When we help others, we build up our own confidence. When we choose to be selfish, we do a disservice to others and our community.

How to build up confidence:

Get enough rest: When we get enough rest, we feel rejuvenated and ready to tackle the day. Our mood is more positive, and we tend to have a more optimistic look for our day. Rest allows us to have more patience with ourselves and with others. Our emotional state is just as important as our physical state.

Love your Look: We tend to feel better about ourselves when we are comfortable and look ready for the day. This can look like so many different things for people. It's how you present yourself to make yourself feel good. I know, for me, I feel better when my hair is colored and I'm wearing makeup. I feel put together. I don't do it for other people. I do it for me. I am also not one of those people who just loves fashion, so I don't have to be in a pantsuit and heels to feel good. I feel best when I am clean cut.

Drink enough water: Believe it or not, we feel best when we are hydrated. Our skin looks brighter and we feel less bloated. You are supposed to drink half your body weight in ounces daily! You also physically can't live without water, so that should say a lot.

Workout: Go on a run, lift some weights, or mix it up—do a combination of cardio and strength training. I used to dread working out despite the amazing benefits. Any kind of physical exercise is great for your mental and physical health. Working out gives you an increase in endorphins and mimics what antidepressants can do you for you. Working out is just a more natural way to feel better.

Choose healthier eating options: This one is hard, for me at least. There is nothing I like better than carbs. I mean, who doesn't like their pasta! I recently had bloodwork done and found out my cholesterol was a little high. That wasn't fun news. I decided it was time to change my eating habits. I reduced the amount of red meat I was eating, choosing other meats such as fish and chicken. I also added a lot of vegetables to my diet. Just after a few weeks, I felt so much better. I felt better physically, and I had a lot more energy than before.

Be conscious of what you put into your body. Everyone has a different body type and not one particular diet will work for everyone. Choose to strive for healthy options.

Walk with your head held high: Have you ever seen a baby who is just starting to sit on their own? Just the other day, I noticed a friend's baby who had just learned to sit up by herself, and oh my goodness, her posture was perfect. I quickly realized how poor adults' postures can be. I don't know if that baby felt confidence in that instance, but she sure looked to be proud of herself. When we walk with a purpose and have our head held high, we are conveying a sense of confidence to the world. Did you know that we tend to notice non-verbal communication before ever speaking to someone? When we avoid negative body language such as slouching, crossing our arms, and crossing our legs, we tell our brains that we are the ones in control. We have the power of building our confidence.

Engage with other people: This one is so important. I can't tell you how many times I have come into contact with people who just don't acknowledge me, or anyone else for that matter. I hate it when you walk into a room and the people there just ignore you and don't have the decency to say hello. It's important to look people in the eye when you are talking to them. It shows that you have respect for them and that you are confident in what you are speaking about. Just remember, when all else fails, talk about the other person and ask questions. When you show you are interested in the other person, you are building rapport and developing positive connections.

Talk positives into your life: On a daily basis, according to science, we have about 50 thousand thoughts and a majority of them are more negative than positive.[1] Think about that for a minute. How in the world can we be successful and confident in ourselves if we speak negative lies and choose to believe them? It's important to be your own advocate, and by advocate, I mean you have to love yourself, take care of yourself, tell yourself you are worthy and beautiful. I laugh sometimes when my kids are driving me crazy, and I just keep reciting "I love my life. I love my life." It's not that I don't love my life, but I'm choosing to speak positively in a stressful situation. Heck, if you have to, post sticky notes all over your mirror or wall or car, with positive statements about yourself.

I could go on and on with more on the list to help build your confidence up, but I think you get the gist. This is a great starting point, and believe me, even these points will take a lot of practice. Your mindset about everything and everyone is essential to your confidence level. Honestly, you can't accomplish much without a certain level of confidence. If we believe we are incompetent or inferior, it will hold us back from what great things life has to offer. So grab the bull by the horns, girl, and barrel through because you are amazing.

Life is Like a Dance

I met my husband back in 2006 when I was in college. I was still a little on the wild side, and he was six years older, so he was a bit more stable and accomplished. He proposed to me in May of 2007, and that's when the amazing wedding planning began. Since I was a little girl, I had dreamed of what my wedding would look like. So, of course, that meant my husband didn't have much say in many of the details.

There was one surprise we had up our sleeves, though. Neither one of us knew how to dance but we wanted our first dance to be memorable, and a friend of ours just happened to be a dance instructor. We kept the dance lessons a secret and practiced for months. Our wedding and reception day rolled around, and we were introduced as

There will be times where struggles come along and you may lose your footing and fall, but that is okay because that is a part of life and a part of the learning process.

Mr. and Mrs. Steven Rowell. I'll never forget our first dance as they played "New York, New York" by Frank Sinatra. My husband and

I gracefully began our choreographed dance as everyone circled around us on the dance floor, cheering. My husband even wore a top hat and cane for a wow effect. It was epic!

As we were beginning our life together as a married couple, I realized that navigating our way through life would forever be like a dance. Things would never move smoothly and flawlessly throughout our entire marriage, let alone our entire lives, but we would navigate them together. In the song "These Days" by Rascal Flatts, it mentions that life can throw you curves, but you can learn to swerve. That's where I am going with this, only we are dancing.

Throughout our lives, we will learn to be a leader. We will also learn that there are times when we need to follow. We will learn that there will be times we need to just learn as we go. The point is to enjoy each step of the way and to not rush. There will be times where struggles come along and you may lose your footing and fall, but that is okay because that is a part of life and apart of the learning process. One of my favorite parts is to improvise. Sometimes, dancing to your own beat creates a magnificent masterpiece that you would have never known was there until you began. Remember, life is not about getting from one place to the other. It is about enjoying each step, each stumble, and each teaching moment along the way.

Remember to be true to yourself and to not live your life to please others.

Life has so many lessons ready for you to learn and teach to others. We go through hard times to strengthen us and make us a better version of ourselves. We learn to have persistence. I hope the people who are ahead of you on your journey will not put you down but encourage and lift you up. And I hope, if you are ahead of other people on their journey, that you will lend a helping hand without expectations. The people below you may be jealous and fear they will never accomplish what you have. Love these people. Love, encourage, and teach.

I want you to know that no one is perfect. Don't even strive to be perfect because you will fall short and only feel awful about yourself. Instead, learn to love yourself where you are in life. Learn to love others where they are in life. Remember, you are good enough and worthy of love. You are worthy to be loved unconditionally.

But you can't and won't be able to do it all, so delegate. Don't feel bad about it. To be successful, you will need to let go of some things and let other people help you. I assure you that people who are moving forward in life do not do it all themselves. They have help and they don't feel bad about it, and neither should you.

Remember to be true to yourself and to not live your life to please others. Of course, help others along the way, but set your own boundaries so that you don't get burnt out. It's never too late to change the course you are on. And remember, when you are true to yourself and don't compromise who you are, you are being the most authentic version of yourself that you can be. Each day, you are better than you were before.

There will be times that life will feel like it is out of your control, and a lot of times, this is true. Try your hardest to look for the positives in each and every situation. Remember to use your coping skills to get you through the toughest of times. Use your tribe, your girls, your best friends to help lift you up in times of need. Let them help you build your confidence back up. And when all else fails, and you are down on your luck, just improvise and Dance It Out, Girl!

WHAT'S YOUR NEXT MOVE?

I hope you enjoyed reading Dance it Out, Girl: Navigating the Mess and Beauty of Motherhood. It was a pleasure to be able to create this book and share it with you. I hope you were able to find inspiration and encouragement as you read through the different chapters.

If you enjoyed reading this book and believe it has the potential to encourage others, here are some things I'd like to ask you to consider...

- Share a positive post about the book on Facebook, Instagram, or other social media, and use #DanceItOutGirl.

- I would also love to connect with you on a more personal level. Please feel free to send me an email at Info@perfectlyimperfectcounseling.com

- Consider ordering a copy of my first book, *Chains Be Broken: Finding Freedom from Cutting, Anxiety, Depression, Anorexia and Suicide.*

- Order extra copies of this book to share with others. To order copies of any of my books or to learn more about the counseling services I offer, go to my website at www.perfectlyimperfectcounseling.com

- Join our mothers Facebook group at Perfectly Imperfect Mama's

Let your journey in healing begin today!

Uncover your true potential. Become who you are meant to be. You are not alone. Life is your journey. Find your passion. Solve everyday issues. Develop more meaningful relationships. Let go of stress and enjoy life more. Healing is your power.

Be empowered! Gain the support you deserve in a safe environment. You can obtain positive growth, healing, and well-being through your counseling experience.

Post-Traumatic Stress Disorder

Self-Injury

Couples Counseling

Family Counseling

Parenting Support

Stress Management

Perfectly Imperfect Counseling

www.perfectlyimperfectcounseling.com

NOTES

Introduction

1)   Proverbs 16:3 (New International Version)

Chapter Three

1)   Psalm 139:14 (NIV)

2)   Wikiquote contributors, "Bernard Baruch," Wikiquote (website), accessed February 2019 , https://en.wikiquote.org/w/index.php?title=Bernard_Baruch&oldid=2598237

Chapter Four

1)   quotefancy contributors, quotefancy's page for Demi Lovato's quote, quotefancy (website), accessed , https://quotefancy.com/quote/793716/Demi-Lovato-In-treatment-all-of-the-negative-things-I-did-were-stripped-away-and-I-had-to

Chapter Five

1)   John 16:33

Chapter Seven

1, 2)   American Pregnancy Association website contributors, "Do I Have A Form Of Postpartum Depression?," American Pregnancy Association, last updated April 8, 2015, https://americanpregnancy.org/first-year-of-life/forms-of-postpartum-depression/

3)   1 John 3:18

4)   quotefancy contributors, quotefancy's page for Anita Moorjani's quote, quotefancy (website), accessed May 2019, https://quotefancy. com/quote/1712065/Anita-Moorjani-Unconditional-Love-is-our-birthright-not-judgment-or-condemnation-and

Chapter Eight

1)   Anonymous quote

2)   Karl Lagerfeld, AZQuotes's page for Karl Lagerfeld's quote, AZQuotes (website), accessed , https://www.azquotes.com/quote/578059

Chapter Nine

1)   Amy Morin, "Depression Statistics Everyone Should Know," Verywell Mind (website), last updated March 21, 2019, https://www.verywell-mind.com/depression-statistics-everyone-should-know-4159056

Chapter Eleven

1)   Stan and Jan Berentstain, The Berenstain Bears and The Truth, New York: Random House, 1983

2)   James E. Faust, "Honesty—a Moral Compass," The Church of Jesus Christ of Latter-day Saints, accessed May 2019, https://www.churchofjesuschrist.org/study/general-conference/1996/10/honesty-a-moral-compass?lang=eng

Chapter Twelve

1)   Genius contributors, "Them Belly Full (But We Hungry)," Genius (website), accessed June 2019, https://genius.com/Bob-marley-and-the-wailers-them-belly-full-but-we-hungry-lyrics

Chapter Thirteen

1)   University of Texas commencement speech, 2014

Chapter Fourteen

1) Jennifer Green, Winning While Losing: The Upside of Heartbreak (Victoria, British Columbia: Friesen Press, 2017).

2) Quote Investigator contributors, "It's Never Too Late To Be What You Might Have Been," Quote Investigator (website), accessed , https:// quoteinvestigator.com/2013/11/24/never-too-late/

Chapter Sixteen

1) David A. Bednar, AZQuotes's page for David A. Bednar's quote, AZQuotes (website), accessed April 2019, https://www.azquotes.com/ quote/689146

Chapter Seventeen

1) Hara Estroff Marano, "Depression Doing the Thinking," Psychology Today, last reviewed June 9, 2019, https://www.psychologytoday.com/ us/articles/200107/depression-doing-the-thinking